Sorting Through
GOD's LOVE

God's Love Story

Belinda F. Payne

Publisher's Note:

Scripture quotations are taken from the King James Version (KJV) of the Holy Bible 1967 Edition of the Scofield Reference Study Bible.

Copyright by Belinda F. Payne
All rights reserved.

ISBN - 978-1-7324670-0-2

ISBN 978-1-7324670-0-2

9 781732 467002 >

Editor: Linda Stubblefield
Cover design, internal formatting & layout: Hemant Lal
Website: www.AaronProductionsIndia.com

DEDICATION

In Loving Memory of our Beautiful Lil Jeff

Jeffrey Alexander Tharpe

March 11, 2003 – August 25, 2018

ACKNOWLEDGMENTS

The writing of *Sorting Through God's Love* has been faith journey. It is with much love and joy that I dedicate this book to my wonderful husband Alvin, who believed in me from the very first time he saw me. Who fell in love with me on the spot and knew he wanted *me* to be his wife. Much love to my beloved family who support my dream and vision to write what the Lord says to me.

I dedicate this book to my son's and their wives and *especially my grandson.*

I dedicate this book to all the people who will read this book and have an "aha" moment with the Holy Spirit.

Most of all I dedicate this book to my parents, sister and brother. Their love, guidance and direction kept me through difficult times, strengthened me when I was weak and challenged me to achieve no matter what obstacles I faced.

Thank you God.

AUTHOR'S NOTE

Through our trials God uses the ultimate and most effective tool to strengthen our faith -*the trial itself*- to produce enduring faithfulness. And yes, this is the evidence of Jehovah Shammah being with us, not only through seasons of joy and prosperity but also during perilous times and persecution.

If we are careful not to interrupt the process we shall come forth mature, complete and perfect in Christ, having learned how to focus on who He is and not what He does.

In the meantime, ask God for wisdom and let endurance have its perfect work. Then and only then will we emerge with unconditional love for the giver of all life, rather than for life itself.

Persecutions, afflictions, which came unto me at Antioch, at Iconium, at Lystra, what persecutions I endured; but out of them all the Lord delivered me. Yea, and all that will live godly in Christ Jesus shall suffer persecution (II Timothy 3:11-12).

INTRODUCTION

"How do I love thee? Let me count the ways." These near immortal words penned by Elizabeth Barrett Browning and published as Sonnet 43 in *Sonnets from the Portuguese* remains an oft-quoted work because of its subject—love. Can you hear God asking you that question: How do I love you? Have you ever wondered about the ways in which God expresses His love for us? How can God whom we have never seen or touched in the flesh possess the ability to transcend His love for us in a way that it is seen, felt, heard and touched by those of us on earth?

Availing ourselves of God's love can be a challenge for even the most astute Bible scholar. How do you process your emotions of fear, frustration and confusion as you sort through your belief system and resolve that God is a God of love? In fact, God is love (I John 4:8). Feeling loved was a challenge for King David as he lived on the run to save his life from the death threat of his own son, Absalom. Feeling loved was a challenge for Job when destruction and calamity struck his household. Feeling loved was a challenge for Joseph as he sat in prison convicted of a crime he did not commit. Availing Himself of God's love was even a challenge for Jesus Christ, God's only begotten Son, as He hung on the cross and died for the sins of all mankind who ever lived and yet had committed no sin.

We are taught that "God loved the world so much that He gave His only begotten Son, that whosoever believes in Him would not perish but they would have eternal life" (John 3:16). We are taught that Christ died that we might have life and that we might have life more abundantly, which means abundance in peace, prosperity, favor, joy, influence and more. This truth means that as an heir to the throne of God, we can experience this abundance on earth. The Bible tells us, *"The earth is the LORD's, and the fulness thereof..."* (Psalm 24:1).

Herein lies the rub: life does not always feel, taste or look like God Almighty loves us. Sometimes we do not know how to define God's love or how to recognize His love when it is expressed.

Discovering the many ways God demonstrates His unconditional love for us and toward us is imperative in the Christian life. God manifests His presence in the lives of ordinary people like *you* and *me* in many ways.

And as you read this book, remember the words of John 3:16: *"For God so loved the world that he...."*

NeNanNe's Porch

CONTENTS

CHAPTER ONE

HALLELUJAH! GOD LOVES *ME!*

"You know, I question if there really is a God. If there is a God, does He love me?"

Some say, "The Bible says, '*God is love.*' If *God is love,* why do I feel so empty inside?"

"If God is *real,* why don't I know Him? How do I get to know God when He is so far away? I can't even see God. I can't touch God. If there is a God, I am not sure of my relationship to Him."

These comments are frequently heard from people today regarding their perception of God. We live in the "*new age,*" - a time which would suggest that the God of the Bible is not the Supreme Being. The "*new age*" would suggest that God is simply "a higher being." Today many people have never even prayed to God. Some have never prayed because they have never been taught to pray. Others simply do not believe that someone is powerful enough to act on behalf of their prayer.

Some say, "If God does exist, He is not a God of love; otherwise, He would not let bad things happen to me."

Others, in their overzealous nature, declare, "God is love; therefore, it matters not how much I violate His laws. After all, God is a God of love; He will surely forgive me when I do wrong."

One of the most complicated and confusing concepts for most human beings to understand and accept is *"God is...."* Man's struggle to understand the reality of *"God is..."* began long ago. In Exodus 3:13 and 14, God told Moses to present himself to the children of Israel as their redeemer, commissioned by God.

Knowing what he was up against, Moses responded to God by saying, "As soon as I tell the children of Israel that You have sent me to them, they will ask me what is the name of this God who has sent you? *God, what shall I tell them?"*

God told Moses to tell the people, *"...I Am* hath sent me unto you" (Exodus 3:14). Absolutely no explanation! No justification! God declared His existence, His authority and His deity simply as *"I Am."*

Many denominations teach only the New Testament Scriptures; therefore, under that teaching, the believer operates solely in New Testament truth, discounting biblical history prior to the birth of Jesus Christ. The accounts and acts of the manifest presence of God in the lives of His people are chiefly recorded in the Old Testament. Although God does manifest Himself through His Son and the Holy Spirit, He still exists by Himself. God possesses His own attributes and character ascribed to *Him* only. So the question you may be pondering at this point is: are God, Jesus Christ and the Holy Spirit one in the same making up the Holy Trinity, or are they individual? The answer is that they are *both*.

Jesus the Christ, you know. The Holy Spirit, you know. But God the Father, you may not know. Genesis chapter 1 verse 1 says, "In the beginning God created the heaven and the earth." The reference of the name "God" in this text in the Hebrew is *Elohim*. It is the first of the names of the Deity of God. *Elohim* means "true God." Simply put it means *God*. God is the Source of all life and intelligence, who is to be worshipped and served by men and angels. The name *Elohim* is a plural noun in form (relating to or composed of more than one member); however, it is singular in meaning when used in Genesis 1:1, referring to the true God.

Deity is defined as "the divineness of God; the greatness of God; God, the Supreme Being; the Creator of the Universe and the Creator of man." An easier way to think of *deity* may be to focus on the divine nature, character, personality or temperament of God. All these divine attributes of God are embodied in God the Son and manifest through God the Holy Spirit. Because these divine attributes are ascribed to God the Father, God the Son and God the Holy Ghost, for most people to see each entity as individuals is a challenge.

The writer of the text makes a distinction in God's deity in verse 26 of the same chapter when he says, "And God said, Let *us* make man in *our* image, after *our* likeness." Elohim is now plurality in deity and provides our first biblical reference to the *Trinity*. To whom was God referring when He said *"our"*? It is clear He was referring to some other person or persons other than Himself when He said "our." Let's go back a few verses. According to Genesis 1:1, Elohim created heaven and earth. Elohim in singular form is speaking in verse 1, and He (God) speaks creation into existence. Yet, it is important to understand Jesus co-existed with God in heaven. We know this because God shifts tenses in verse 26 when He begins to speak of Himself as more than one member. God's name Elohim is used as a plural noun. Who are the other members? The use of His name Elohim in this context as a plural noun suggests the existence of the Trinity, even in the beginning of time. The Trinity represents God the Father, God the Son and God the Holy Spirit. Yet God is careful to make a distinction in the Trinity.

Throughout the first five books of the Old Testament (the Pentateuch), God begins to reveal His distinct person apart from Jesus and the Holy Spirit to His people by His names. He is also *Shammah* — "Present," *Sabaoth* — "Host," *Jireh* — "Provider," *Rapha* — "Healer," *Adonai* — "Lord," *Shaddai* — "Strengthener" and many more. *Remember,* Jesus had not come to earth during the days of the writings of Old Testament; God dealt directly with His people. God still desires to make Himself known to us in intimate ways. Intimacy with God increases our personal knowledge of who God is. God manifests Himself to His people through His various names.

The revelation of who God is to His people is just as important in the New Testament as it was in the Old Testament. Whenever Jesus performs an act, He always points back to God as His source of power. Jesus wanted us to know God reveals His divine attributes and His acts according to His mighty names. Jesus knew that He received God's blessings, and God's people would be blessed with all spiritual blessings through the manifestation of God by God's disclosing intimate knowledge of Himself in our experiences, relationships, nature, and inheritance and even in our sufferings. The apostle Paul prayed that God would give us the spirit of wisdom and the revelation in the *knowledge of Him* through His Son. We are able to see and understand God through His Son.

The Bible continues to make a resounding declaration of God's existence apart from that of His Son. How do I know that? Look at Ephesians 1:15-20, which says,

"Wherefore, I also, after I heard of your faith in the Lord Jesus, and love unto all the saints, Cease not to give thanks for you, making mention of you in my prayers: That the God of our Lord Jesus Christ, the Father of glory, may give unto you the spirit of wisdom and revelation in the knowledge of *him,* the eyes of your understanding being enlightened; that ye may know what is the hope of *His* calling, and what the riches of the glory of *His* inheritance in the saints, and what is the exceeding greatness of *His* power toward us who believe, according to the working of *His* mighty power, Which *he* wrought in Christ, when *he* raised him at his own right hand in the heavenly places."

Notice that Paul makes a clear distinction between God and Jesus throughout the text, and he also ascribes the power to raise Jesus from the dead to *God.* All power exists in the sovereign God, and that power is manifested in and through His Son Jesus Christ in the New Testament. In John 6:29, Jesus told the people, "This is the work of God, that ye believe on him whom he hath sent." God chose to manifest His power in Jesus to validate the authenticity of Jesus and the authoritative work of Christ. Paul recognized, even though Jesus and God were of the Trinity, that they were individual. Understanding the principle of who God is was so important that Paul prayed that heartfelt prayer in Ephesians 1:15-20, that we as believers would come into the understanding of who God is, as Jesus knew Him to be. Jesus not only knew God as His Father, He also knew God as Elohim—*God alone*. As we examine the lives of those in the Bible, we will discover how they came to know God as Elohim and how you also may come to know Him in the same way.

When we talk about *knowing* God, we will do well to understand the various names through which God reveals Himself. A few of those names were addressed earlier. Let's look at another name of God: the Hebrew name of God *Olam* means "everlasting; eternal duration of the being of God; *of secret or hidden things.*" In this name, indefinite time or age come together. There is no beginning and no ending. Genesis 1:1 says, "In the beginning God created the heaven and the earth." This verse is a declaration of God's existence. It is not a philosophic argument for His existence. He is the God whose wisdom has divided all time and eternity into the mystery of successive ages or dispensations as we see them in the Bible.

According to Genesis 1:28, God said man was to subdue the earth and have dominion over every living thing that moved upon the earth. In other words, God commanded man to take possession and have authority over his environment. God has designed our existence such that it is a natural God-given desire within us to seek knowledge and revelation of the creation. That is why man is always searching to understand what many refer to as Mother Nature.

Recognizing that man did not begin life knowing all the secrets of the universe in which he lived, or those hidden things of God is important to understand. Ephesians 3:1-5 says,

"For this cause I, Paul, the prisoner of Jesus Christ for you Gentiles—If ye have heard of the dispensation of the grace of God which is given me toward you, How that by revelation he made known unto me the mystery (as I wrote before in few words, By which when ye read, ye may understand my knowledge in the mystery of Christ) Which in other ages was not made known unto the sons of men, as it is now revealed unto his holy apostles and prophets by the Spirit."

This text gives special reference to God's name *Olam,* which means "there are secret or hidden things about God that we have yet to understand." We have yet to experience all of God's divine greatness. These hidden truths in Scripture are only understood by revelation from God to whom God chooses. When God created man, He created man with a limited knowledge of the nature of God and His creation. God chose to keep back or reserve exposing His total deity to man. Instead He reveals tiny portions of His greatness and His nature for specific future use and or special purposes that will bring Him glory at appointed times. Deuteronomy 29:29 says, "The secret *things belong* unto the Lord our God; but those *things which are* revealed *belong* unto us and to our children forever, that *we* may do all the words of this law." Once God reveals a truth in His Word to you, it remains in your knowledge forever, and God expects you to obey the instruction or commandments you have learned. Whether you accept or reject that truth, it still remains a truth, and you are still held accountable.

God also wants to have an intimate relationship with us. The children of Israel gained greater knowledge of God through His names. As a result, they began to have an intimate relationship with God as they learned more about His character and His power demonstrated through His names.

God is the same yesterday, today and forever (Hebrews 13:8). The criteria required to know God for the people of God in the Old Testament, is still required for the Gentile nation today. God is not a respecter of persons. God chooses to reserve the revelation of Himself to those who will seek Him with all of their heart—no matter who they are.

Deuteronomy 4:29 says, "*But if from there* thou shalt seek the LORD thy God, thou shalt find him, if thou seek him with all thy heart and with all thy soul." The important element of the text that makes the outcome of the provision to knowing God, one that is conditional is "*But if from there….*" In other words, God says at some point in your life after your last *"I've-had-enough"* experience, if you would make the decision to seek Him with all your heart and soul, you will find *Him*. Proverbs 8:35 says, "For whoso findeth me findeth life...." Once you find God, then you must get to *know* God. Getting to know God is a process not an event. John 17:3 states, "And this is life eternal, that they might know thee, the only true God...." When you find God, you begin to gain knowledge of who God is. His hidden truths are revealed to you. His Word becomes a personal revelation to you through the Holy Spirit.

Understanding God's sovereignty, supremacy and individuality in order to understand *God's love for you* is important. God's love is unconditional. God not only is a God of love in His divine character, *but God is love in His divine nature*. That you embrace this truth in order to *sort through* the manifest presence of God's love in your life, relationships and circumstances is of vital importance.

So why is it a challenge for most people to accept the fact that God does not place conditions on His love and that *Elohim (God alone)* loves them unconditionally? Sometimes the blows a man or a woman sustain in their lifetime cause them to feel they are unloved. Maybe a parent or someone that a person trusted told them they were unlovable. In some cases, feeling unloved is the result of abandonment and abuse in early childhood. These acts left the residue of hate, shame and embarrassment resulting in marred imprints of an undefined and conditional love.

Perhaps you have never been told *"God loves you,"* so let me be the first to tell you. *"Hallelujah*, God loves *you*! God loves you through God the Father, God the Son and God the Holy Spirit." Sometimes we need an affirmation of a promise or a revelation given to us. So wherever you are currently, I want you to find a mirror, look yourself in the eye and say, *"Hallelujah! God loves me!"*

Although this is only the first step, it will be the most significant step to move out of your "fixed" way of thinking. Now you can stop "looking for love in all the wrong places." If you are looking for love and find love, you will find God. If you are looking for God and find

God, you will find love. Maybe you have never found God or love because you have been looking in all the wrong places.

Sorting through God's love may seem like a complicated process. The concept is complicated for you, the unbeliever, who may not even be aware that you are searching for something. Perhaps you may feel you can never be forgiven; however, many believers live their entire sanctified lives failing to understand God's unconditional and abiding love. You may be asking, "How can I sort through that which I don't even understand? Where do I even begin?"

Sorting through a tangible pile in search of a specific item is not unusual; however, searching through the intangible to find a treasure seems not only odd, but to some, virtually impossible. How can a man or woman search through spiritual concepts and gain an understanding of how God's love is manifest in his or her daily routines?

"Jesus loves me this I know, for the Bible tells me so." You may have learned this song as a child in Sunday school or Vacation Bible School. You learned Jesus Christ was God's only son. Jesus came in the form of a babe wrapped in swaddling clothing and laid in a manger on Christmas morning.

You learned that one day Jesus was crucified. The Bible says He was crucified and hung on the cross for the sins of all mankind. The story reads that Jesus Christ rose from the grave three days after His crucifixion and lives in heaven with His Father.

Wow! What a great little song, and what a wonderful story! So what's the point? You may be saying, "I thought the point was to learn God loves me. So why are we talking about Jesus' loving me? What about the answer to all those questions about sorting through an intangible spiritual concept to discover the love of God?"

Let me share a story that may help you understand. I was brought up in a Baptist church. I was baptized by the age of nine, and I have remained active in church all my life. I know the song, and I believe the story. But somewhere around the age of thirty-five, I began to experience a sense of restlessness in my spirit. This was very confusing because I had no idea why I was restless.

It took me about two years to figure out what was going on with me. I thought I needed a new job or a new house. Maybe I needed time to myself, which was not going to happen as I was a wife and the mother of two active adolescent sons, as well as being active in several ministries at our church. Nothing seemed to make me happy or bring contentment. This was not something that would have been evident to others. I had no intention of letting anyone know what was going on with me. *It's an awful thing to pretend to have joy and contentment,* nonetheless I did it.

I gradually stopped spending time with God in my clothes (prayer) closet, as I had done regularly. When I think back, I can imagine God's looking at me from heaven, shaking His head saying, "Tsk, tsk, tsk; this girl really needs rescuing." I think the Lord finally got tired of my whirlwind state, and He spoke. At that point I started to listen.

I went back to my prayer closet and began to spend time with God seeking His face, His presence and His answers to my prayers. This testimony may sound phony, but it really happened.

One day when I was in my prayer closet crying out to God, the Holy Spirit revealed to me why I was restless. I had an unmet longing and a need to know the Father Himself. I began to understand the meaning of the Scripture that says, *"As the deer panteth after the water brooks, so panteth my soul after thee, O God"* (Psalm 42:1).

My soul was simply crying out to have the personal relationship and communion with God that it was designed and created to have, and nothing could fill this void but Him—*not even His Son.* I did not understand this yearning for many years. It was a simple need, yet I had not learned how to fulfill the need.

I remember crying out to God, "I know Your Son, but I don't know You!" I did not understand I was responsible for spending time alone with God. I have been taught to pray in Jesus' name and to spend time getting to know Jesus. The only thing about that teaching is that it is simply incomplete. I needed to understand so much more about my relationship with God. I spent years developing an intimate relationship with Jesus never understanding I could have as intimate a relationship with God as the one I had with His Son!

Of course, I believed in God, but there was a gap in our relationship. We had a distant relationship. I had reverential fear for God, but it was not intimate. I did not know God reveals Himself through His names. I did not know God had various names that represented His character and nature. Most importantly, I had not come to know God as *Elohim*. I had a good understanding of biblical principles and the relationship of the Holy Trinity, God the Father, God the Son and God the Holy Spirit, but I had developed a distorted view of God; I only saw Him as *my heavenly Father*. I did not see Him as *Elohim*.

I felt God is too big for us to have a relationship with Him. That's why He sent His Son. Don't we let Jesus do all the work in meeting with the Father on our behalf? After all He is our intercessor, isn't He?

I spent 35 years of worshipping and praising God with a distorted view of God in the life of the believer and my responsibility as His daughter in establishing a loving intimate relationship with Him.

Can you understand the story now? Here's the revelation: *my search for the intangible was a result of a spiritual longing and barrenness in my soul that was impacting my daily routine. My soul was longing to experience an intimate relationship with God and gain greater revelation of God and His love for me. I had developed an intimate relationship with Jesus in the person of the God the Son. I had developed an intimate relationship with God in the person of God as my heavenly Father, but I had not developed an intimate relationship with God as Elohim.*

Many people spend their lives developing an intimate relationship with Jesus, but they fail to develop an intimate relationship with *Elohim*. They recognize God as their heavenly Father in role and responsibility, but they never recognize God as *Elohim* and never really understand His deity is the essence of who He is. When you come into the knowledge and revelation of God loves you for you, you begin to see God as Jesus saw Him. The Bible reads in John 3:16, *"For God so loved the world that he gave his only begotten Son, that whosoever believeth in him should not perish, but have everlasting life."* God sent His Son to save the world—not to condemn the world.

In this text, we not only see God as a loving Father willing to give His only Son as a ransom to the entire world; we see the greatness of God's power to reconcile us to Him, so that each one of us can have a personal and intimate relationship with God through His Son.

I John 4:10 says, *"Herein is love, not that we loved God, but that he loved us, and sent his Son to be the propitiation* [the sacrifice, or one that would take the place of] *for our sins."* God made a way to completely satisfy the need of men and women looking for self-redemption rather than God's redemption. He made it possible that we whom He has redeemed could always experience His love.

Because God loves us, it is impossible for Him to leave us in our lost state. Man was created by God to express His love, with the expectation that we would give love back to Him.

Proverbs 8:17 says, *"I love those who love me; and those that seek me early shall find me."* Jeremiah 31:3 says, *"The LORD hath appeared of old unto me saying, Yea, I have loved thee with an everlasting love; therefore with lovingkindness have I drawn thee."*

Even though we sin and fall short of the will of God through our deeds, *God still loves us.* God is not vindictive or vengeful as we are when we have been wronged.

God shows His mercy and deems the believer *righteous* ("to be all that He demands and requires") because of the sacrificial atonement through the death of His Son, Jesus Christ.

God loves *you* so much that everything possible that could be done was completed in His Son on the cross so that you may now have a personal and intimate relationship not only with the Son, but also with the Father.

So come to the Father who loves you and accepts you just the way you are. No masks, no pretending. God already knows you in your worst state, and He still chooses to love you unconditionally. Jesus wants you to get to know the Father, *Jehovah God,* as He does. You are God's sons and daughters and precious to God. Receive His love for you and walk in the newness of your revelation.

Come, come, *come…* He is patiently waiting.

CHAPTER TWO

THE TESTING OF DELAY

"Now a certain man was sick, *named* Lazarus…When Jesus heard *that*, he said, This sickness is not unto death, but for the glory of God…When he had heard therefore, that he was sick, *he abode two days still in the same place where he was*" (John 11:1, 4, 6).

Waiting for the manifest presence of God in our prayers and our circumstances can be quite frustrating, especially when it seems like God is late or He has chosen not to show up at all. King David was no stranger to being tested by God. He knew what it felt like to wait under duress for God to reveal Himself. David cried out to God in the thirteenth number of Psalm verse 1: *"How long wilt thou forget me, O Lord? forever? how long wilt thou hide thy face from me?"*

God may use several forms of discipline to get our attention. One form of discipline is that which perfects us unto greater fruit bearing through divine stimuli from God. This form of discipline is often manifested in our lives through what is known as the discipline of delay. The object of this delay is either to produce Godly character in us or to produce within us a consistent pattern of behavior in response to circumstances in our life.

Why would God's directive be that Jesus delay His arrival until all hope of Lazarus' recovery was lost? Not only did his sickness prevail, but it eventually led to Lazarus' death. Jesus had been informed several days earlier of His dear friend's grave illness. Yet He chose not to come to Lazarus' aid or even acknowledge the sisters' concern. Mary and Martha experienced God's love through the discipline of delay.

Mary, Martha and Lazarus were dear loved ones of Jesus. They *always* took care of Jesus when He was in town. Mary had wiped His feet with her precious oil, her tears and her long beautiful hair.

Yet when word was sent to Jesus, He chose not to hasten to their call. Why would a loving and kind God choose to teach two sisters an important lesson through *the discipline of delay*? Based on what we have read, they certainly appeared to be "good" Christians who lived their lives in the will of God. Yet it was God's will that they endure delay—even unto the death of their only brother.

Take a look at another ordinary man who experienced God's love through the discipline of delay. When you were a young child, you may have read a story or seen a picture of a guy in a den or cave-like atmosphere with hungry lions looking on him. This picture gave you the idea that there was no way of escape for this poor fellow. It appeared it would be only a matter of time before this guy would be eaten alive by the lions. Well, that guy in the lion's den was Daniel, a man of great integrity. His love for God was so great he would not compromise his relationship with God under any circumstances. Daniel was willing to die for his convictions. He was wholly committed to living a lifestyle that honored God's Word and commandments.

Daniel was the man who knelt and prayed aloud with his face pointed toward an open window three times a day. Even after he had been ordered to cease praying or be put to death, Daniel prayed and gave thanks to God as always. Daniel maintained his devotion to God against the opposition of those who threatened to take his life. He continued to kneel and pray three times a day and give thanks to God as he had always done.

As a result of his steadfast commitment, jealous men arose and conspired against Daniel with a plan to set him up to be thrown into the lions' den. These men knew Daniel was devoted to prayer and God, so they used Daniel's prayer life as a means of entrapment.

These ruthless men convinced the king to establish a decree that would forbid anyone from praying or asking a petition of any man or god, except the king, and if caught doing so, they would be thrown into the den of lions. The expectation of these worthless men was that Daniel would be eaten alive by the lions for serving God. But God had other plans. God protected Daniel while he was in the den, and the lions did not touch Daniel. God delivered Daniel out of that lions' den. You will find the account of this testing in Daniel chapter 6.

On another occasion of testing in Daniel chapter 1, Daniel was appointed the choice selection of the king's food and wine for his daily meals. Daniel defied King Nebuchadnezzar's orders by not eating the food and wine that he was told to eat. Daniel chose not to defile his body with these rich delicacies. He chose instead to eat only vegetables and drink water. This act was in direct violation of the law. Notwithstanding, Daniel could have been put to death for making this decision. Daniel was but a youth at this time, but he had established a relationship with God early in his life. Even as a youth, Daniel's convictions were strong, and he maintained his loyalty to God. God gave Daniel favor with those who ruled over him, and he was allowed to eat the diet that he knew was more appropriate for him rather than that which would have harmed his body. Even as a youth, God will test you.

You may be thinking, "I thought God was all-powerful. Why would God let something this awful happen to a man who had committed his life to God? I thought God was a God of love." Surely God could have done something to prevent Daniel from being thrown in the den of lions in the first place. Why would God allow Daniel to be thrown into the lions' den because of his convictions to serve *Elohim*? Why would God allow ruthless men to put His own child in harm's way? But as we have read God *did* in fact choose to exercise His sovereign will, and He allowed Daniel to face the threat of death and imprisonment under unusual circumstances all because He loved Daniel.

As you can see, even Daniel experienced God's *discipline of delay*. God did not step in and thwart the plan of these mischievous men. Neither did God keep Daniel from being put in the lions' den.

It seems like those experiences should have been enough testing by God for one man. Now we find Daniel under still another test in chapter 10 of the book of Daniel. The text says:

"Then said he unto me, Fear not, Daniel: for from the first day that thou didst set thine heart to understand, and chasten thyself before thy God, thy words were heard, and I am come for thy words. But the prince of the kingdom of Persia withstood me one and twenty days...and I remained there with the kings of Persia" (Daniel 10:10-13).

This scene is quite different from the other two accounts we have read. In both previous instances, the tests were against his physical body. These tests were imposed upon him because of the action of others in order to produce greater Godly character in Daniel as well as create a more intimate relationship between Daniel and God. This intimate relationship was developed through God's discipline of delay.

In Daniel chapter 10, we find Daniel had been praying and fasting several weeks, seeking God regarding the revelation of vision God had given him. Daniel understood the vision, but it had not been revealed to him when the manifestation of the vision would occur. During his period of fasting and prayer, Daniel saw a vision; and in the vision, the features of a man (angel) appeared to him. The angel spoke to Daniel who then fell into a deep sleep. A hand touched him and set him upon his knees and the palms of his hands, and he began to speak to him.

God took Daniel through yet another test unlike the physical testing he had previously encountered. In this test Daniel did not face physical obstacles or opposition from men. This test was in His spirit and in his mind. To understand God's will concerning his vision, Daniel had placed his body under subjection of the Holy Spirit through prayer and fasting during which time he had this spiritual encounter with God through yet another vision. In the vision, an angel told Daniel he was greatly beloved by God—so much so that he (the angel) has been sent by God to deliver to Daniel a personal message. As a matter of fact, the holy angel who was sent to minister to Daniel was caught up in a war in the heavens with unholy angels. So great a quest was ensued by the unholy angels to prevent the holy angel from reaching Daniel that Michael the archangel, one of the chief princes, was sent to help the holy angel fight against the unholy angels.

These unholy angels did all they could to prevent Daniel from receiving the word of God through the holy angel. So Daniel waited 21 days from the day he first prayed until the day the angel of the Lord appeared unto him. His strength had waxed cold. Daniel could hardly stand upright in the presence of the angel of the Lord as the angel gave him the word from the God. Once the message was delivered, the angel returned to fight with the prince of Persia. The holy angel was only able to get away from the battle with the help of Michael just long enough to deliver a word from the Lord.

One principle that you would do well to accept if you are going to be victorious in your Christian walk is to accept the fact that God either allows us to go through adversity (His permissive will) or He will send (His divine will) us through adversity. As harsh as that statement may sound, it is a biblical truth. In the case of Daniel, *that he suffers was divinely planned.* In the case of Mary and Martha, God's permissive will allowed two sisters to experience pain and suffering through delay. What do you do when it seems like God has purposed that you suffer and prolonged your deliverance? You put yourself in remembrance of what the promises of God are concerning your battle. Then you put God in remembrance of the promises He has made to His children as He commands us to do in Isaiah 43:26 when God says, "Put me in remembrance: let us plead together: declare thou, that thou mayest be justified."

I am confident that during Daniel's 21 days of prayer and fasting, he was pleading with God. Even when his flesh became weak, his spirit prevailed; he held on to God's promises despite his overwhelming condition. I am confident Mary and Martha were earnestly praying as they waited.

God makes an oath and a promise to us in Numbers 23:19 that whatever He has said or spoken He will make good of His Word. God is not man, and God is incapable of lying. Daniel knew God would be faithful to His Word, and He would not forsake him in his time of need.

Even Jesus Christ experienced God's *discipline of delay* when He hung on the cross. He too, in His flesh, cried out to the Father, asking God why He had forsaken Him at such a time like this. "And at the ninth hour Jesus cried with a loud voice, saying, Eloi, Eloi, lama sabachthani? which is, being interpreted, My God, my God, why hast thou forsaken me?" (Mark 15:34). He had been beaten all night long. The flesh had been torn from His body as He was scourged. Even Jesus revealed His innermost emotions under testing in that if it were His choice, He would much rather the bitter cup and taste of sin and death pass from Him. As Jesus agonized in the Mount of Olives, he prayed, "Saying, Father, if thou be willing, remove this cup from me: nevertheless not my will, but thine, be done" (Luke 22:42).

Yet He knew the Father's love was so great it could never be quarantined in one man, *Himself.* God's love had to be manifest in the lives of all mankind.

Had God not delayed His response to the cries of His only Son and responded in ways that demonstrated He was only thinking of Himself and His Son, we would be doomed for eternal damnation in hell.

If God had chosen to remove His Son from the cross, the entire world would still be lost. Surely there had to be a better way for God to get this foundational truth across without sacrificing His only Son. *Why is it so important that God use the method of delay as a form of discipline to develop Godly character in His children? Because God's rule or standard of subjecting us to rigorous spiritual boot camp to produce a specific character or pattern of behavior that governs our belief system, our responses to our circumstances and our lifestyle is paramount to God.* God knows He can accomplish His purpose and develop our character through delay of the manifestation of His answers to our prayers.

What happens when God decides to delay His manifest presence in our circumstances? Why would God use this method of delaying His response to our prayers as a means of discipline? *Who said we needed to be disciplined anyway?*

The wise book of Proverbs tells us to train up a child in the way he should go. So why should God be restricted in training His children in the way they should go, yet we be given the liberty to train our children in the way they should go? Are we bigger than God? Who are we to tell God what is the best method of training and discipline to develop Godly character in us?

Many times, we see discipline as a cause-and-effect relationship. When we were small children, our parents disciplined us when we were disobedient. That form of discipline was often a nice solid pat across our hind part. So we associate discipline with measures taken to rid us of bad behavior.

I believe God uses *the discipline of delay* for several other reasons.

For divine correction and reprimand.

To enlarge our vision of Him.

To increase our faith.

To develop our spiritual ears that they become sensitive to His voice and His voice only.

To teach us to pray.

To show us the ways of God.

To reveal His love for us and to us in every situation and circumstance we go through in life.

To teach us the meaning of the names of God and their relevance to every issue we face in our lives, as the children of Israel learned to use these names in times of distress and during periods of praise and worship.

To equip us for opposition and obstacles that we will face in everyday situations.

To help us understand the fullness of His love for us.

We, on the other hand, respond to God's discipline of delay in one of three ways.

1. We simply give up on God and lose faith in God.

2. We decide to *assist* God and begin to facilitate the process by creating the desired outcome. As a result, we find ourselves living outside of God's will.

3. We realign ourselves, and we check to see if we have sinned. If we have sinned, we confess, repent, turn away from sin and begin to look for the face of God. Or once we know our problem is not a result of sin or broken fellowship with God, we are able to understand that our season of discipline is a test of our faith that will glorify God.

We are taught to trust in the Lord always and not to rely on our human understanding to work out our problems.

Sometimes we wait only a few hours or a few days for God's answer to our prayers, but I have learned that when God is really developing our character, we may wait upon the manifestation of the presence of God in our prayers *for several years.*

I have come to believe God's Word as He declared through Jesus when Lazarus was ill. Jesus said, "*...but for the glory of God, that the Son of God might be glorified thereby*" (John 11:4). *You see, God is more interested in developing our character than He is our reputation. God will do whatever it* *takes to accomplish His objective, including delaying His purpose for the season of discipline that we are in.*

Through the process of becoming disciplined in your prayer life and in your worship time with the Father, *God is glorified.* When you become an intercessory prayer-warrior establishing a consistent time to meet with God and by keeping your flesh in subjection to the spirit as Paul admonished us to do, *God is glorified.*

Is *the discipline of delay* necessary? You bet it is. It's worth your whole life and the quality of the life you will live as a believer. Your ability or inability to accept *God's method of divine training to produce Godly character* in you is a matter of life and death. God's training is designed to propel and equip you for your divine destiny. God's boot camp will give you the power and ability to maximize your potential in every endeavor you encounter. The divine principle of *delay* is a form of discipline that shapes your entire belief system. This is why so many believers do not live the abundant life for which Christ sacrificed His life. They are unable to accept God's divine method of discipline. People simply do not like waiting for God to answer their prayers.

Choose ye this day to *wait* upon the manifestation of the promises of God. The safest place is always in the will of God. What we must learn to do is *wait in God's will*, not only wait *on* God's will. I believe there are differences in *our* actions when we wait *in* God's will versus when we wait *on* God's will.

Most believers do not recognize there is a difference, and therein lies the challenge. When we wait *in* God's will, we give God permission to act as the sovereign Agent in our circumstances as we position ourselves in total submission to Him. It is not a place; it is a position—*a position of total submission.* The waiting may take several hours, several days, several months or several years. Yet the believer waiting *in* God's will remains faithful to God despite his circumstances. When you wait in God's will, you are willing to do whatever God tells you to do even when you don't agree with or understand the instruction He gives you because you trust God.

When we wait *on* God's will, we typically wait *for* God to fix our circumstances. As we wait *on* God, we may find ourselves doing one of four things:

1. We sit back and relax with the attitude if it does not work out, it just was not meant to happen.

2. We take on an attitude of worrying and becoming anxious about our circumstances.

3. We advise God how we want the job done and what His completion time line is since we have other matters hinged on God's ability to meet our deadline.

4. We decide the wait is too long, and we take matters into our own hands to help God get the job done. *Wrong!*

Listen, no matter how long it takes, you've got to trust God and wait *in* the will of God. *Waiting upon God to show up in your circumstances becomes the disciplining factor. The act of waiting in the spirit (in His will) is a methodical means by which God uses to produce obedience in the life of the believer.* Whether or not you believe this, God is very methodical. It may appear that the route He is taking is off course, but God knows what He is doing. Some of you reading that statement may be feeling a little provoked at this point because you do not agree with the course God has you on. However, it is important to understand that while you wait *in* the will of God, you must keep your focus and stay busy ministering unto the Lord.

When your season of waiting, testing and proving has been accomplished, you will come forth as pure gold. God is faithful! God is all knowing! Jeremiah 29:11 says, "For I know the thoughts that I think toward you, saith the LORD, thoughts of peace, and not of evil, to give you an expended end [a future and a hope]". You will be a vessel that has been tested by the fires of life and proven to be faithful and worthy of your calling. If you are sincere about this Christian walk, you will *walk through the fire to reach your expected end!*

So don't get so haughty and puffed up in self-righteousness as Job did. God reminded him of Whom he was speaking when He said to Job:

"Shall he that contendeth with the Almighty instruct him? he that reproveth God, let him answer it." Then Job answered the LORD, and said, Behold, *I am vile; what shall I answer thee? I will lay mine hand upon my mouth...but I will proceed no further"* (Job 40:2-5).

Even when we have done no wrong, God has the right to discipline (subject us to spiritual boot camp) us unto greater fruit-bearing ability for His glory. God's desire is that we bear *much* fruit. God knows fruit bearing can only occur *in His will*. God knows we will engage many physical battles that can only be fought *and* won in the spiritual realm.

God knows "...we wrestle not against flesh and blood, but against principalities, against powers, against rulers of the darkness of this world, against spiritual wickedness in high places" (Ephesians 6:12).

This is one of those hard sayings because our issues are processed through our flesh receptors or our natural senses. So we typically see our battles as physical encounters of opposition from other people. However, these principalities and high places are territories and airways occupied by evil spirits (Satan). They are not people or things that we can see or touch. God knew this fight would be a lifelong battle. He knew this fight would require we become soldiers ready and equipped for battle at a moment's notice, a soldier who would take authority over the Enemy.

So we were provided with the whole armor of God, so we would be able to withstand in the evil day. We are to gird our loins with the truth. We are to be people of integrity and honor. God knew if we misrepresented the truth of the gospel, we would reproduce spiritual dwarfs and this error of doctrine would retard the growth of the church of Jesus Christ.

We are to cover our breast with the breastplate of righteousness so that our heart and emotions would be protected from those that would seek to take advantage of our love and our emotions. We are told to shod our feet with the preparation of the gospel of peace, the good news that Jesus Christ born of a virgin died and rose with all power in His hands because God knew we would have to walk through the valley of the shadow of death. and we should fear no evil that His presence was with us, that His peace which passeth all understanding would keep our hearts as we keep our minds stayed on Him. God knew we would need to take the shield of faith because many would reject Jesus Christ through us because we *re*present a standard they are not ready to live by, and we would need to protect ourselves from their fiery darts.

God knew we would need a head covering, so He told us to cover our head with the helmet of salvation, so we could protect and guard our mind. He knew the mind is the Devil's playground. He knew the battle begins and ends in the mind. So we would have to guard our heart through our thoughts. We need the helmet, so we don't develop strongholds based on distorted beliefs channeled through our brains which have been processed out of emotions.

God knew that we would have to fend off the Enemy, so He gave us a sword; this sword would be His presence manifest in the Holy Spirit. The Holy Spirit would be with us, in us and upon us, representing the abiding presence of God in the believer. He knew that we alone would never be able to win a lost soul to Christ, so He told us to take the Word of God because this Word is living and powerful. It pierces and divides asunder the soul and spirit and the joints and marrow of man. The Word is a discerner of the thoughts and the intents of a man's heart.

There is nothing that can be hidden from the Word. John said in John 1:1, "In the beginning was the Word, and the Word was with God, and the Word was God." You can't hide anything from Jesus who is the Word. So He tells us to take His Word so the Word will reveal those things men do in the dark that they may be known in the light. We will be equipped to know what we are dealing with when we are in the battle. God knew we would be in a battle for our life, and He expects us to be victorious.

God sent His Word to reach and touch the life of every man, woman, boy and girl—every sinner and every saint. He sent His Word to us through a virgin birth, and that Word suffered bled and died. But that Word rose and ascended to the Father in heaven. God loves us just that much! So much so that He is willing to chasten us through His spiritual boot camp to make sure when we have done all, *we are able to stand* and see the salvation of the Lord in our life and in our circumstances. Hallelujah! I could really shout right here! I think I need to take a praise break. Hallelujah! Hallelujah! Yes, hallelujah! Blessed be the name of the Lord! Glory to God!

Okay, I've got my composure back! Now let me ask you a question: were you the kind of child who always had to have the last word with your parents? Well, I'd think twice about pursuing your rights to have the last word with God.

Certainly, God expects and invites us to have a two-way dialogue with Him. After all, that is the definition of prayer. But some of us take it just a *little* too far and find ourselves up a tree and out on a limb. As a matter of fact, let me just tell you straight up! You are on your own when you choose to exercise your *last word rights* with God when they extend past the definition of reverential prayer.

I've done that only once with God, and the experience left me completely void of His anointing. I could not figure out what was wrong. There was no anointing in my prayers or my praise and worship for approximately two weeks.

I'll explain what I mean. I had a few angry words with my husband, and the encounter left me somewhat bitter. A few weeks had gone by, and one day as I sat and talked with my husband, he reminded me of something I had said in anger to him a few weeks earlier. (Actually, the Holy Spirit had already brought this to my attention, but I ignored Him) My words had hurt my husband's feelings. As my husband spoke, the Holy Spirit immediately reminded me that it was because of that haughty and ungodly statement I had made to my husband that He had taken away His anointing from me.

34

I had basically told my husband that because I had a favored position with God I could do what I wanted, and it was none of his business. *Talk about pride and lifted up in self-righteousness!* Job didn't have anything on me. *Well,* God showed me my real position.

I felt the Holy Spirit encouraging me to keep my mouth closed before I opened my mouth during our argument. *Actually I don't think you can define this as an argument since I was the only one doing the talking.*

Anyway, being a woman, and you know how we can just go on and on about something when we feel we are right, I chose to ignore the Holy Spirit's leading. I chose to speak my mind. I had to get the last word.

I knew my husband was right as he reminded me of how harsh I had spoken to him. I confessed and repented to God as well as to my husband. And God restored me; He placed His anointing back into my life. I knew it because His peace came over me instantly, and I felt the restoration of His anointing. God moved me back into my *right* position *(now humbled position)* of harmonious fellowship with Him that very moment.

Now that was unspeakable joy! You know, I love God so much, and I had been miserable those few weeks without His anointing. Although God was still protecting me and meeting my needs, I had no power in my prayers, praise and worship. That is the emptiest feeling I have ever experienced.

I never want to experience that type of separation from God ever again. Nothing is worth separating you from God's anointing. *The price is too high. The burden is too great.*

I was totally void of the will of God all because I refused to be *disciplined by delay* under God's loving hand of correction. I wanted things my way. I wanted it now, and I felt I had earned a high enough position of favor with God that I could get it. *Wrong!*

God told me very clearly, *"Just as I had to turn My back on My Son because He took on sin, I would turn My back on you. Don't ever think more highly of yourself than you ought."* You better believe I got the message. We don't have enough grace and mercy in our whole body that could even come close to paying the down payment needed to get our anointing back. Neither can you earn enough grace and mercy in your lifetime— no matter what you did.

My prayer to God was that He would ever keep that experience before me to buffer me and to keep me in the way that He has prepared for me. Even if it means disciplining me by delaying His answers to my prayers as the means to develop Godly character in me for His glory.

Amen.

CHAPTER THREE

UNDERSTANDING GOD'S LOVE

It's a different kind of love. His ways are unsearchable. His thoughts are higher than our thoughts. His purposes, divine. His love is everlasting.

Did you know that it's God's will that we suffer? *Well,* great *Guglamuuglia!* What kind of loving God is that? Yeah, I know that's not a real word. But it's a word my favorite uncle would always say, and it fits right here. The Bible says in Isaiah 30:20, "And though the Lord *give* you the bread of *adversity,* and the water of *affliction,* yet shall not thy teachers be removed into a corner any more, but thine eyes shall see thy teachers."

Well, with that message, who in their right mind would want any part of a God like that? I would! Why not? He knows my past, present and future. He knows me better than anyone else on earth. He knew me before I was formed in my mother's womb. Need more reasons? Okay, here goes. My destiny rests in His hands. He knows my expected end. He knows the reason for my birth. He knows what I think before it registers as a cognizant thought in my mind.

God demonstrates His redemptive love and reconciliation through our suffering. We also experience God's blessings and restoration through suffering. Even through sickness and deprivation we see God's salvation in healing and forgiveness. If we allow God to teach us in our suffering, we will enlarge our vision of God and the power of God to work in our lives and our circumstances. Need more convincing? Let's look at a man named Hosea—a man with feelings and emotions just like you and me—who was handpicked by God to demonstrate God's redemptive love for mankind.

Let's examine God's love. Although God demonstrates His love for us in numerous ways, I want to look at how God demonstrates His love **toward** us, **for** us and **in** us in three ways.

Number One:

We are loved through God's redemptive love and reconciliation.

"The word of the LORD that came unto Hosea…And the LORD said to Hosea, Go, take unto thee a wife of whoredom(s) and children of whoredom(s)… So, he went and took Gomer…" (Hosea 1:1–3).

From the text God clearly knew what type of relationship Hosea would have with Gomer. He knew that Hosea would have a marriage filled with adultery. Yet, *he would experience a divine marriage ordained by God.*

The Bible tells us not to be unequally yoked. Nonetheless Hosea married Gomer, and God *permitted* him to do so. God clearly explained exactly what type of wife Hosea would marry. God knew Gomer would be a mother who would *not* train up her children in the right way. God knew Gomer would spend more time in the streets than she would at home taking care of her husband and children.

The thought of going into a permanent relationship with someone with the foreknowledge of their future unfaithfulness and lack of respect for you seems unreal.

To help us understand His love for us, God parallels Hosea's experience with His relationship to Israel during a period of her unfaithfulness to Him. This comparison gives us a good illustration of how God felt and feels when His people place others before Him. God uses Hosea's marriage to demonstrate His love for us.

We spoke earlier about man being made in God's image and that God gives man free will. Sometimes exercising our *free will* often finds us out of the *will* of God and stuck out on a tree limb that is ready to break.

God demonstrated His power through His redemptive love. God wanted to show His people that He would still love them and take them back even when they sought intimate relations with those who did not love or care for them as He did. God created man so that man would worship Him as Lord and seek a loving intimate relationship with Him. Instead, man chose to have an intimate relationship with anything and anyone but God. Did you know our natural affections are designed to meet what satisfies or brings gratification to our flesh or what makes us feel good?

So, it was with Hosea's wife. Gomer found gratification of the flesh through sexual pleasure. As a result, she continually gave herself to other men and defiled her body. Hosea was hurt and shamed by her behavior. Hosea wanted Gomer to come home on time to feed their children. He wanted a wife who loved him and gave her affections to him alone. He wanted a wife whom his children could call blessed and one that he could praise. I believe Hosea would have preferred that Gomer not work outside the home at all, much less have a working profession of a prostitute. How painful it must have been to look into her eyes day after day, knowing she had been with other lovers. Did Gomer see the hurt in her husband's eyes? Did she feel his pain? Hosea begged Gomer to stop prostituting her body. Hosea wanted to have an intimate relationship with his beloved wife.

Nonetheless, Gomer chose to look for fulfillment and gratification in all the wrong places, and we are still looking for fulfillment in all the wrong places today. We look for fulfillment through our jobs, relationships, possessions, self-indulgence and more. Eventually, Gomer's lifestyle of prostitution and lascivious living caught up with her, and she was placed on the auction block to be sold to the highest bidder.

"Then said the LORD unto me, Go yet, love a woman beloved of her friend, yet an adulteress, according to the love of the love of the LORD toward the children of Israel, who look to other gods, and love flagons of wine. So I bought her for myself for fifteen pieces of silver, and for an homer of barley, and an half homer of barley. And I said unto her, Thou shalt abide for me many days; thou shalt not play the harlot, and thou shalt not be for another man: so will I also be for thee" (Hosea 3:1-3).

"I will heal their backsliding; I will love them freely; for mine anger is turned away from him. I will be as the dew unto Israel: he shall grow as the lily, and cast forth his roots like Lebanon. His branches shall spread, and his beauty shall be as the olive tree, and his smell as Lebanon" (Hosea 14:4-6).

In the text God instructs Hosea to purchase Gomer back to himself through an auction and to love her with the same love God has for His people, Israel. It is expected that Gomer would repent of her unfaithfulness. God parallels Israel's unfaithfulness to that of Gomer, and He looks for Israel to repent of her unfaithfulness to Him. God's love for His people is parallel to that of Hosea's love of redemption and reconciliation for Gomer.

Despite the idolatrous ways of Israel's worshiping and loving other gods, God seeks to redeem Israel and reconcile His people to Him. So God chooses to illustrate His love through the heart of a man named Hosea. In returning, Gomer is analogous to Israel in experiencing healing from backsliding, as well as love and future blessing through restoration. God's divine love is manifested **in** His redemption and reconciliation.

Did you know God grieves when we are unfaithful to Him? Have you ever looked into the Father's eyes? Did you feel His pain? Have you allowed yourself to see His hurt because of your unfaithfulness? If you did, then I know you experienced a spiritual transformation and reunion instantly with God. There is no way we can look into the Father's eyes and not have our heart transformed.

A look into the eyes of the Father brings repentance. The problem is we don't look out of fear and shame, and that is a ploy of the Enemy to keep you captive to sin.

God will allow *(His permissive will)* you to experience betrayal by a trusted friend and the unfaithfulness of your spouse to demonstrate His redemptive love for you to draw you closer to Himself.

God loved Hosea, and He loves you with a love that is so powerful it is greater than life itself! *You* are God's greatest creation. God did not permit Hosea to marry Gomer as a means of punishment or to say, "I told you so."

Hosea's tragic experience is used as a basis to portray God's own relation to Israel during a period of unfaithfulness. We too will experience God in unusual ways during times in which we are unfaithful to God.

In His permissive will God allowed Hosea to be in a marriage with Gomer to demonstrate what it feels like when we, His people, are unfaithful to Him. He also demonstrated His love **for** us by developing Hosea's heart to love with the love of God even when he had been forsaken and betrayed by the one he loved most.

Even when we *willfully* make the wrong choice, God demonstrates His love **towards** us, and delivers us out of the mess in which we have entangled ourselves. *Now that's what I call mercy!*

The key to living a victorious life is to learn the way of escape. I know this may sound like a cliché, but this is a biblical truth. The way of escape will always be found *in God's will for your life.*

God desires that you know Him. God desires that you know His will for your life. He desires that you experience His love and that you can extend the love of God toward others. Even when we continue to be unfaithful, God's love remains constant. God does not regulate or adjust His love according to your deeds. *His love is constant.* There is nothing you can do to make God love you more, and there is nothing you can do to make Him love you less. The thief on the cross was a perfect example of this very love. *Hallelujah! God loves you!*

Number Two:

We are loved through God's blessing and restoration.

Let's look at the life of Job to understand the expression of God's love through blessing and restoration. You should be familiar with Job. Job had a family life that was the opposite of Hosea's. Job had a loving and faithful wife. He had wonderful, obedient children. All his family's financial needs were secured; as a matter of fact, Job's wife did not have a job outside of the home.

There were servants all around, cattle in the fields and the barns were full. Hey, and let's not forget that Job served the Lord through prayer and lived as a godly man and a man of integrity in all of his dealings. What more could God ask for in a servant like Job?

Well, God did ask for more. Because of a contest between God and Satan, God allowed Job to be tested. Although God declared Job righteous, God knew that Job had a greater capacity for spiritual growth and development. God chose to allow Job to experience spiritual maturation through testing. If we were to ask Job, I am sure he would say there was nothing in his life that needed to be improved, and he probably felt he was mature in his relationship with God. *Well,* God didn't ask. God will do what He wants to do when He wants to do it and with whomever He chooses to do it through. Get my point?

So let's just get over this because you will never win with your logic, and God is not required to explain what seems illogical when dealing with you! God is a God of logic and order! I know that sounds like a contradiction of the previous statement, but it is not. God's ways simply appear illogical to us because we can't understand how God thinks.

"For my thoughts are not your thoughts, neither are your ways my ways, saith the Lord. For as the heavens are higher than the earth, so are my ways higher than your ways, and my thoughts than your thoughts" (Isaiah 55:8, 9).

So don't try to read God's mind. Instead learn to trust His hand and His heart.

Man can only begin to understand the logic (mysteries) of God when he begins to have an intimate relationship with God. Face it. *God does not have to get your permission to demonstrate His love in your life.*

So the test begins. As we say today, *"It's on now!"* Some of you know the story, and if you don't, just keep reading. Job begins to lose everything, and I mean *everything!*

It was just a regular day in the house of Job. All was well when suddenly Job received news that the Sabeans have attacked, taking all his livestock and killing the servants caring for livestock barring the one servant left alive to bear witness of the event. While this servant was still speaking, a second servant rushed in and explained to Job that fire had fallen from heaven and burned up the sheep and those servants, and he was the lone servant left alive to bear witness to Job. Then a third servant hurried in proclaiming they had suffered attack and slaughter by the Chaldeans. The Chaldeans had taken all of the camels and killed the servants by sword, and he was the sole witness left to bear the news to Job. Then a fourth servant rushed in while the third servant was still speaking. The servant told Job that all his children were gathered in the eldest brother's house, and a great wind came from the wilderness and smote the four corners of the house. As a result the house collapsed upon the children, killing them all. At that point Job tore off his mantle, shaved his head, fell to the ground and worshipped God.

To make matters worse, all this death, destruction and devastation occurred within the same day. Job's life goes from the peak of prosperity and comfort to a valley of despair and desolation all within twenty-four hours. God chose to exercise His providential right to allow Job *(there's that permissive will again)* to face challenges of seemingly un-survivable odds at the hand of *Satan*.

Then if that weren't enough, a few days later Job's body was afflicted with boils from the crown of his head to the soul of his feet. *Talk about pain!* God allowed Job to endure testing throughout 38 chapters before He even acknowledged His presence to Job. Not only did God allow Job to experience testing, God had the nerve and the audacity to chasten Job during his suffering saying, "Then the LORD answered Job out of the whirlwind, and said, Who is this that dakeneth counsel by words without knowledge?" (Job 38:1, 2).

Job responded to God, and God continued to speak to Job saying, "Moreover, the LORD and said, Shall he that contendeth with the Almighty instruct *him*? he that reproveth God, let him answer it" (Job 40:1, 2). God challenged Job because He knew Job was still responding to His questions based on how he saw himself and not how God sees him.

Can you imagine that? *P.S.* We are still talking about love so don't get lost in the drama!

God sees what we cannot see, and He knows more about us than we will ever admit to ourselves about ourselves. God knew that in all of Job's righteousness greater purification was required because Job was still falling short of God's plan. There was an element of Job's character that did not fit God's character.

It was *pride*! Job had a prideful heart. Job had too much pride in his relationship with God. Sometimes we can get lifted in pride because of the love and favor of God has shown toward us, and we lose touch with others around us. As close as Job was to God, his pride separated him from God. Job said, "My righteousness I hold fast, and I will not let it go: my heart shall not reproach me as long as I live" (Job 27:6).

This pride factor becomes a hindrance in our relationship with God and with others. I believe that's what happened in the life of Job. God strategically positioned Job to experience life through a contest with Satan. Was it really just a contest with Satan to prove Job's loyalty and commitment to God? Did God have another purpose for recommending His servant Job to be tried at the hands of the enemy? One fact is sure; because of the contest, Job's vision of God was enlarged. God used the process of purification and restoration to open Job's spiritual eyes.

Although Job prayed and worshiped God daily, Job's experiences with God had not revealed God's true holiness. Job's experience of suffering, devastation and loss took his worship and prayer life to another level—a level he never knew was available to him.

In his season of pain and suffering, Job's wife told him to just curse God and die. Along come Job's three best friends to sit alongside of him. They sat with Job from chapter 2 through chapter 42. You know how well-meaning friends are, don't you? They can always tell *you* what you are doing wrong and how *you* can correct *your* situation. Friends are always ready to give you *their* advice. Job's friends were convinced he must have done something wrong to deserve what had happened. *After all, bad things don't happen to good people.* So they sat with Job for days and days.

The dialogue continues through 39 chapters between Job's justifying himself before his friends and his friends acting as judge and jury over his case. *P.S. His friends had already found him guilty as charged.*

The book of Job contains 42 chapters, and not until the forty-second chapter did Job recognize his own futility in comparison to the power of the living God. Job did not see himself as God saw him until God revealed Himself to Job in his entire splendor, power and glory as God Almighty. *Then* Job made an interesting, but heart-wrenching, confession in this final chapter. Job acknowledged God's sovereignty and holiness:

*"Then Job answered the L*ORD*, and said, I know that thou canst do everything, and no thought can be withheld from thee. Who is he that hideth counsel without knowledge? therefore have I uttered that which I understood not; things too wonderful for me, which I knew not"* (Job 42:1-3).

He confessed that he had uttered that which he really did not understand. *You know how it is.* You hear people say "Glory!" so you begin to say "Glory!" You really don't know what it means, but it seems befitting to say during worship services. It just sounds good.

What I like most about the entire book of Job is noted in verse five of chapter 42. Job says, *"I have heard of thee by the hearing of the ear: but now mine eye seeth thee"* (Job 42:5). You see, Job knew God at a distance, and that's what I meant when I said I had a distant relationship with God.

His was not an intimate relationship with God. Job thought he knew *Elohim*, but he only knew *of Elohim*. Even though he prayed and worshiped daily, his relationship with God was not intimate.

Sure, He loved God. But he loved Him because of what he had heard about Him. He loved God because of what others had said in their testimonies about the living God. He loved God because of things God had done for him. But somewhere between chapter one and chapter forty-two Job developed a personal and intimate relationship with God. He no longer saw God through the experiences of others; he had seen God through the eyes of his own experiences.

Remember, we read in Ephesians 1:17 and 18 that God's greatest desire is to impart within us the spirit of wisdom and revelation in the knowledge of Him that the eyes of our understanding would be enlightened and that we would know the hope of Christ's calling. It is the will of God that we receive the riches we are entitled to through our inheritance in God. When we have a personal and intimate relationship with God, *we will experience His mighty power*. That's what happened to Job between chapters 1 and 42! Job experienced God and His mighty power! Now he understood God's love through *his* own experience.

Job proclaimed, "Wherefore I abhor myself, and repent in dust and ashes" (Job 42:6). Job never repented because of his suffering. Job repented of his ways when he comprehends the holiness of God. Job saw himself in contrast to God's holiness. Only then did Job see that he was no better than the chief sinner in the land. He was no better than his friends. That's when the veil of doom and despair lifted from Job's life. The test was over. Job had passed the test.

The prophet Isaiah said, "But we are all as an unclean thing, and all our righteousnesses are as filthy rags; and we all do fade as a leaf;

and our iniquities, like the wind, have taken us away" (Isaiah 64:6). I believe Isaiah included Job in this statement. Even Job's righteousness was as a filthy rag in the sight of God.

Not until Job demonstrated *sincere compassion* for his well-meaning friends did his circumstances change. Job 42:10 reads, *"And the LORD turned the captivity of Job, when he prayed for his friends: also the LORD gave Job twice as much as he had before."* When Job became an intercessor on behalf of others, God turned his situation around.

Maybe that's what God is waiting for you to do before He will turn your situation around. Perhaps God is waiting for you to stop being selfish and begin spending time praying for someone else.

Once Job saw God in his suffering, he sought God for more than a distant relationship. He repented. He humbled himself. He worshiped God in his current state. He didn't say, "I'll worship God after He delivers me from my problems." Job worshipped God before he received deliverance from his problems. Because of his suffering, he saw the holiness of God.

God was waiting for Job to recognize the holiness of God with a contrite heart before He would demonstrate His love through *blessing* and *restoration.* Job learned to trust God and to serve with a greater passion for God and sincere compassion for others. God chose to exercise His sovereign rights in a contest with Satan.

We will never understand all the reasons why God chooses to do what He does, and God is not required to provide us with an explanation. But we do learn Job's suffering is corrective rather than penal. God used this test to refine Job's character by enlarging Job's vision of God's divine holiness.

Can devastation, blessing and *restoration serve* as a means of God's demonstrating His love **for** us, **toward** us and **in** us? YES! *Yeah, right!* Most people would not define that as love, but God may choose to demonstrate His love for us by positioning us to suffer. Our failure to receive or accept the ways and movement of God's hand in our lives will break our fellowship with God. God demonstrates His love *toward* us and *for* us through our suffering as He did through the lives of Hosea and Job. Just as God did in the life of Job, He will do in our lives. God will turn our suffering into blessings. He will restore that which was lost or taken away with greater benefits than that which we had before our season of affliction and suffering.

God wants us to come out of our season of suffering with a personal revelation and knowledge of who He is. He is Shalom, our peace; Jehovah-Shammah, the Lord Present with us in our circumstances. He is *I Am*—Yahweh.

Yes, sometimes it's difficult to understand God's way of demonstrating His love in our lives when we look at our circumstances. But God is a Spirit and God is sovereign, and He uses divine ways to bring about blessings and restoration in our life that turn our hearts toward Him so that we may see His heart of love for us.

God expects us to take the likeness of Christ Jesus upon ourselves and begin to look at our experiences through our spiritual eyes as Jesus did on the cross.

In all of his sufferings Job still loved and worshiped God. I don't doubt that at some point in his season of suffering Job wanted to tell his three best friends and his non-supportive wife to "take a long hike off a short pier." But Job finally gained a spiritual understanding of the ways of God. He took his eyes off his losses, the people around him and his painful condition, but he never took his eyes off the Father. He cried, and he even became angry at times, but he never turned his back on God. God never took His eyes off of Job or turned His back on him either, *and God will never take His eye off of you.*

What an awesome love story between God and His child! Won't you receive the love of God in your heart today? Confess your ways to the Father and expect to receive immediate restoration and God's blessings.

Number Three:

We are loved through God's healing and forgiveness.

And then...there are people! *GGGEEeeeeezzz, Louissseeee...* Yeah, I know that's not a real word; *just work with me!* Did you know that everything would be okay if it weren't for people? You wouldn't get angry. You wouldn't have to lie. You wouldn't have to go through those changes you go through.

Now that's funny because someone out there looks at you and thinks the same thing. "If it weren't for (your name), I would be all right." Can you imagine what the world would be like without people? Well, neither can God. That's why He made us.

For some reason, God seems to think we are worth our existence. Good or bad, great or small, if you are reading this book you are still alive, and God seeks to reveal Himself to you in a personable way.

Let's look at Joseph, the beloved son of Jacob, also known as *Israel*. He did not ask to be born. He did not ask to be favored by his dad; it just happened. By the time he knew who he was and that he was the favored son, the cement was hardened. I'll tell you who did know he was favored; his brothers knew, and they weren't happy about his status. We soon learn Joseph's favor and fortune turn out to be his downfall and plan for his demise.

*Talk about bad luck...*Joseph inherited his fate, *didn't he?* Let's not be so quick to feel sorry for Joseph. If you do not know the story, refer to the biblical text found in Genesis chapters 37 through 50. Now you know this guy must have been very important if one book of the Bible devotes 14 chapters to his life.

Here's a quick summary of these 14 chapters. Joseph was highly favored by his father Jacob because Joseph was the son of Rachel, the wife Jacob loved more than any of his other wives. Rachel bore Jacob, also known as Israel, two sons in his old age, Joseph and Benjamin. In fact, Rachel died giving birth to Benjamin.

In today's language you might say Joseph and Benjamin were overprotected and *spoiled*. Now tell me, have you ever met a child or adult who did not know he was spoiled and did not take advantage of his position? I'm sure Joseph took advantage of this with his father.

I'll share a modern-day experience of what I mean. I grew up with a little brother who learned how to take advantage of his position as baby of the house. He would use the power of his tongue to scream (at the top of his lungs, of course), *"They're aggravating me"* whenever he wanted to get my older sister or me in trouble. So what do you think my mother's response was? "Leave him alone!" He always waited for the opportune moment to scream. We could have been provoking him the same way when my mother was not at home, and he would not scream out. I wanted to knock his block off when he did that. His actions simply reiterated to me that he was spoiled. P.S. I have outgrown that, and my brother is my best friend. *No, really, I have.*

I think I have a glimpse of what Joseph's brothers felt like. The Bible tells us that Joseph's brothers hated him. Joseph was seventeen years old, and he acted like a spy. He would always check on his brothers to see what they were doing when they were away from the house, and then run back and tell their father. The relationship between Joseph and his brothers was so bad his brothers rarely spoke to him. Then to top things off, Joseph had a dream. He told his brothers about the dream.

Joseph told them he had had a dream that their sheaves were bowing to his sheaf. His brothers retorted asking him if he thought he was going to have rule and authority over them. His brothers thought, *How dare he? Who does he think he is?*

Because of the dream and the words he had spoken over them, they hated him all the more. Even when he shared the dream with his father, his father was not receptive at the thought that he too would be subject to bowing down to Joseph. Yet his father took notice of the saying, but his brothers envied him.

Shouldn't Joseph have recognized he was the source of the problem? Shouldn't Joseph have known he was intentionally contributing to division between him and his brothers? He chose not to believe he was the source, and so do we when we are the source of the problem. Life is always easier when we don't have to accept responsibility for our actions.

Joseph was hated and rejected by his brothers, and they plotted to take his life; however, the plot changed because of Joseph's brother Reuben. Reuben admonishes the other brothers not to shed blood and to place Joseph in a pit in the wilderness instead. Reuben had every intention of secretly returning to the pit to remove his brother and take him home, but his plan was foiled. While Reuben was away from the camp, the other brothers discussed a way of ridding themselves of Joseph by selling him to the Ishmaelites, but someone beat them to the punch. Midianite merchantmen came along the path and drew Joseph out of the pit and sold him to a band of Ishmaelites for twenty pieces of silver. Joseph was taken into Egypt. Reuben returned to the pit to find Joseph gone, and Reuben was devastated.

The brothers must now devise another plot. A story must be fabricated to tell their father of Joseph's disappearance. The favored coat of many colors Joseph's father had given him was stained with the blood of a kid goat by Joseph's brothers and brought to their father. The deceit grew and grew. Once you begin to lie, you will likely feel compelled to keep lying. After seeing his son's coat covered with blood, Jacob, Joseph's father, assumed the worst and believed a beast had devoured Joseph. The brothers said nothing to change his assumption.

It would appear that Joseph's life goes downhill from here. Joseph was drawn up from the pit and sold into slavery in Egypt to Potiphar, an officer of Pharaoh, for twenty pieces of silver. God was with Joseph, and he began to prosper at everything he did. As a result, Potiphar made Joseph overseer of his house, and all that he had was put into Joseph's hands. God blessed Potiphar for Joseph's sake. God blessed all that Potiphar had in his house as well as in the field. The only thing that Joseph did not have control over was the food Potiphar ate and Potiphar's wife.

Now Joseph was very handsome, and Potiphar's wife began to take an interest in Joseph. She asked Joseph to make love to her every time she saw him. Joseph, being an honorable and godly man, refused her advances.

Potiphar's wife was insulted by his continued refusal to make love to her. One day during one of her advances, Joseph fled from her presence and, in his doing so, she grabbed his garment and called the guards. She fabricated a lie and told the guards that Joseph had attempted to rape her, but when she had screamed in protest, he left his garment with her and ran away. She kept the garment as evidence, and upon her husband's return, she showed it to Potiphar and lied to him, saying Joseph had tried to have his way with her.

Potiphar brought Joseph in before him and questioned Joseph's loyalty. His wrath was kindled against Joseph. Potiphar had Joseph thrown into prison.

Oddly enough, Joseph found favor again. God was with Joseph. This time the favor was with the keeper of the prison. So the prison keeper gave Joseph charge of all the prisoners. Everything Joseph did or touched while in prison prospered. As we would say today, "He's got the Midas touch."

In addition to good looks, Joseph was also blessed with spiritual gifts. He was able to interpret dreams. Joseph was asked to interpret the dreams of the king's chief butler and chief baker who were in prison with him. He told the chief butler that his dream meant he would be restored to his butlership by the king. He told the chief baker that his dream meant that he would be hanged from a tree. Joseph told the butler and the baker how he was sold into slavery and that he had been wrongly imprisoned. Joseph then asked each of them to remember what he had done for them by interpreting their dreams, and whenever they go before the king to make mention of him.

Now the opportunity arrived for the chief baker and the chief butler to make good on their promise to Joseph. The king's birthday was three days after Joseph interpreted their dreams, and the king decided to throw a feast to all his servants in celebration of his birthday.

Pharaoh had the chief butler and the chief baker removed from prison and brought to the palace. He restored the butler to his butlership, and he hanged the chief baker just as Joseph had prophesied.

Two years passed, and the butler had yet to speak a word to Pharaoh on Joseph's behalf. As we say today, "Out of sight, out of mind." Then Pharaoh had a dream and sought for someone to interpret the dream. He called all of the magicians and wise men of Egypt, but none could interpret the king's dream. The butler stepped up and acknowledged to the king that he had made a pledge to Joseph. He told the king that Joseph had interpreted his dream as well as the chief baker's dream when they were in prison together and what Joseph had prophesied came to pass.

Pharaoh sent for Joseph, and Pharaoh told Joseph of his dream that no one else had been able to interpret. Joseph told Pharaoh that the dream was from God, showing Pharaoh what He was about to do in the land of Egypt. He told Pharaoh that the land was going to experience seven years of plenty followed by seven years of famine.

Joseph told Pharaoh that he was to seek out a discreet and wise man and to set him over all the land of Egypt. Joseph told Pharaoh about God's strategic plan and instructions in order to survive the seven years of famine.

Once again, in spite of his condition of bondage and what appeared to be bad luck, God was with Joseph, and he found favor with Pharaoh. Pharaoh recognized the presence of God in Joseph and restored Joseph by making him ruler over his household and over all of Egypt. The only person Joseph would not have rule over was Pharaoh himself. *Even the enemies of God know and recognize God in the people of God.*

In spite of his previous imprisonment, God showed Pharaoh that there was no one else more discreet or wiser than Joseph. Pharaoh took the ring off his own finger and gave it to Joseph to wear, symbolizing the power and authority he had given to Joseph. He arrayed Joseph in fine linen and put gold about his neck. He gave Joseph a chariot to ride in, second in line to him.

Pharaoh later made a decree, stating no man in Egypt could lift his hand or foot without Joseph's permission. *Good God almighty!* Can you believe that? Talk about being *"the man"*! These people fell just shy of having to get Joseph's permission to breathe. Look at the power and authority God was giving Joseph. God made the king dream a dream that required Joseph as the interpreter. God has divine ways of promoting us. Who would have thought that God would use the interpretation of a dream as the means by which to elevate His servant? That's what God meant in the Scripture when He said, "His ways are not our ways." Joseph was the man for the moment. He moved from the pit to the prison to the palace.

At the age of thirty, Joseph ranked high in majesty, power and glory. He did as God had instructed and gathered food from the field and grain as the sand of the sea. He married and had two sons. Soon the famine came as predicted, and the people of Egypt as well as other countries came into Egypt seeking food.

Pharaoh sent the people to Joseph, who opened the storehouses and began to sell grain.

Jacob, Joseph's father, learned of available grain in Egypt, and he sent his ten sons (Joseph's brothers) to Egypt to buy grain. Jacob kept one son, Benjamin, (Joseph's brother by Rachel) at home for fear of losing him to some form of mischief.

Once the brothers arrived in Egypt, they were sent to Joseph, who recognized his brothers. However, they did not recognize Joseph. After all, he had taken on the look of the Egyptian culture.

Joseph had learned the language and taken on the dialect of the Egyptians. He questioned the brothers about their background, their origin and their father. He accused them of being spies. Joseph put them to a test and did not allow them to return home with the grain. He put them all in jail, returning in three days and giving them instructions that one of them will be required to stay in prison while the others returned home with the grain. They were to get their brother out of prison under the condition they returned with their youngest brother, Benjamin.

The nine brothers began to talk among themselves, recalling the wrong they had committed more than ten years ago. They felt the duress that had befallen them was a result of what they had done to Joseph. Reuben reminded them that he had warned them not to sin against Joseph, but they had not listened. All the while Joseph was listening to their conversation, but they did not know he understood what they were saying because he had only spoken to them through an interpreter. Joseph turned and walked away from them and began to weep. He regained his composure and returned to them again. Joseph decided all but Simeon could be released to return to Canaan with the grain they have purchased. As they were traveling to Canaan, one of them opened his sack to feed his ass and he discovered money had been secretly returned in his sack. He told his brothers of his discovery, and they all became afraid.

Once the brothers arrived home, they told their father, Jacob, all that had happened on their trip. As they emptied their sacks in front of their father, they find that each brother's money was, in fact, in his sack as well. Jacob also became afraid. Their father was reminded of his loss in Joseph and now Simeon, so he refused to let them take Benjamin back to Egypt. Reuben even told Jacob that he would offer the lives of his two sons if he failed to bring back Benjamin and Simeon. Jacob refused his offer.

After a while, the grain that the brothers had brought back to Canaan ran out, and Jacob instructed them to return to Egypt to buy more grain.

Judah spoke up and reminded Jacob that "the man" who sold them the grain said they should not see his face again except their brother Benjamin was with them. They would be unable to buy grain since he was the only man in all of Egypt who could sell them grain.

Jacob asked, "Why did you tell him you had a younger brother in the first place?"

They explained to their father that "the man" had asked them very specific questions about their kindred, their father and if they had another brother. They never expected "the man" to ask them to bring their brother to him.

Jacob was finally persuaded of Judah. He told Judah to take the best fruits in the land, balm, honey, spices, myrrh, nuts, and almonds and double the money, plus the money that they had found in their sacks. Warned, Benjamin returned with them also. Jacob prepared himself for the worse in the event his son Benjamin was not returned. The brothers set out once again on their journey to Egypt, this time with Benjamin.

When the brothers arrived in Egypt with Benjamin, they were ordered to Joseph's house. They were unaware they had been invited to Joseph's house for a feast. They believed that the invitation was a result of the previous misfortune of finding money in their sacks. Joseph's steward greeted them at the door.

They made their confession to the steward about the money in the sacks as well as the money they had brought with them to make new purchases. The steward told them that he was the one who put the money in their sacks. He brought Simeon out to them. They were then brought into Joseph's house and made ready to present themselves before Joseph.

Joseph arrived, and the brothers unknowingly *bowed themselves to the ground before him* and gave him the presents as he had predicted they would in his dream. Remember the dream about the brother's sheaves bowing to Joseph's sheaves? The manifestation of the dream had come to pass. This too was a form of God's discipline of delay. God did not tell Joseph how long it would be before the dream would be manifested. But God is faithful to His Word, and Joseph's brothers were bowing and giving him honor, something they vowed never to do.

What Joseph did not realize at the time that he had told the brothers of the dream was the cost of his divine elevation and appointment. He did not know how and when he would be elevated. He had no idea his position of authority and honor would separate him from his family. He did not understand greater fruit bearing would cost so much and require complete self-denial. He did not understand that with responsibility came great sacrifice. Joseph is not alone in this thinking. We too often fail to understand that when God chooses to use us for kingdom business, it's not what it appears to the natural eye. We make the mistake of judging those who have risen to visible levels of popular ministries on airways and media as having "arrived." We do not understand the cost that they have paid for the work of the ministry that ultimately glorifies God.

Even in the midst of his excitement at seeing his brothers, Joseph remained cool, calm and collected. He asked of the welfare of their father. They responded that their father was in good health, and they bowed down to Joseph again. Then Joseph saw Benjamin, *his* mother's son. He asked if he were the younger brother of whom they had spoken in their previous visit.

Knowing this was the only brother with whom he shared the same mother, Joseph's heart became so full of emotion, he could no longer contain himself. Joseph hastily left the room, entered his chambers and wept. Upon regaining his composure, he returns to his brothers. The bread was set out for them to eat. As was the custom of the Egyptians, Joseph did not sit at the same table with his Hebrew brothers, for doing so would have been an abomination to the Egyptians. Joseph sat his brothers at a separate table before him according to their ages beginning with the firstborn.

Joseph dined with his brothers, never revealing his true identity. In the morning Joseph had their bags packed with grain, and once again their money returned.

Joseph then ordered his steward to put his silver cup in the sack of the youngest brother, Benjamin. He waited until the brothers were gone out of the city and had his steward to go after them to ask them why they had done evil after all the good that had been done to them. The brothers were bewildered, so they pledged the life of the one where the evidence was found as ransom.

They each searched their sacks, and the silver cup was found in Benjamin's sack. They were distraught for they had made a binding pledge with Joseph's steward, and Benjamin must be sacrificed. They all returned to Egypt and fell to the ground before Joseph with shame and embarrassment.

Judah spoke on behalf of all the brothers and told Joseph the words of their father. For the first time since Joseph had been sold into slavery, he heard of his father's love and longing for him. He heard of the sorrow and pain his father had suffered because of his disappearance.

He learned that his father had requited himself unto death if his brothers returned to Canaan without Benjamin. So Judah offered himself in lieu of Benjamin, for he knew he would not be able to bear seeing his father's pain.

At this point Joseph lost total control of his emotions, and he began to cry hysterically right in front of everyone. He had everyone leave the room except his brothers, and he made himself known to his brothers. He began to cry so loudly that he was heard throughout Pharaoh's house. He told his brothers that he is Joseph, and he asked again about their father. The brothers were terrified and unable to speak as a result of this new revelation. He brought them close to him and reassured them he would not harm them.

In Genesis 45:5-8, Joseph told his brothers:

"Now therefore be not grieved, nor angry with yourselves, that ye sold me hither; for God did send me before you to preserve life...And God sent me before you to preserve you a posterity in the earth, and to save your lives by a great deliverance. So now it was not you that sent me hither, **but God....**"

In chapter 50, the final chapter of Genesis, Jacob, Joseph's father, died. Once again Joseph's brothers become afraid, fearing the only reason Joseph had not recompensed them for the evil they had done to him was because their father was still living. They thought, *Surely now that our father is dead, Joseph will pay us back of all the evil we have done.* Once again, they devised a scheme and lied to Joseph, telling him that their father had commanded that he forgive his brothers of their sins and trespasses.

Joseph began to weep. He knew his brothers were lying to him. He was hurt that after all this time his brothers still did not trust him. His brothers bowed before him and offered themselves as his servants.

Earlier we read of the account of Job's experience; now let's see how this account compares with Joseph's. Joseph made a statement that I believe well represents Job's position as well. He asked, "...am I in the place of God?" Talk about being humbled by your experiences.

Job and Joseph had experienced God's favor and His hand of discipline. They had both suffered with a pride syndrome that needed to be buffered before God could use them for His glory. They each had to be abased before they could recognize the sovereignty of Almighty God. Did you notice the Scripture indicates that they never sinned against God in their suffering? As a matter of fact, Job 1:20 says, "Then Job arose...and worshiped" after receiving the bad news from his servants. Verse 22 says, "In all this Job sinned not, nor charged God foolishly." Job never accused or blamed God for his condition or losses.

After years of scorn, suffering and sacrifice, Joseph emerged with greater love and praise for God. He was grateful that God chose him to be the vessel to save an entire nation. In Genesis 45:5 he said, "...

for God did send me...." In verse 7 he said, "And God sent me before you to preserve you a posterity in the earth..." In verse 8 he said, "So now, it was not you that sent me here, but God: and he hath made me a father to Pharaoh, and lord of all his house, and a ruler throughout all the land of Egypt." Notice the word *sent* is used several times throughout his declaration. Believe or not, it is good that we suffer *in the will of God.* I will address this principle more in chapter five.

That Joseph would suffer for the glory of God was God's divine will. In spite of being scorned and rejected in the past, Joseph saw the hand and purpose of God in his circumstances, and he gave God praise for every battle he had faced.

His life had gone from the pit to the prison to the palace. If Joseph were here today, he might say, *"It's all good."*

Joseph told his brothers, "But as for you, ye thought evil against me; **but God** meant it unto good, to bring to pass, as it is this day, to save much people alive" (Genesis 50:20).

God moved in the life of Joseph, Job, Daniel, Hosea, Mary and Martha with the common goal that they would come into the knowledge of Him through his expression of love **for, toward** and **in** them through their experiences. As a result of their boot-camp training, they developed an intimate relationship with God. I believe they would agree with Job when he said, "...therefore have I uttered that which I understood not; things too wonderful for me, which I knew not. Wherefore I abhor myself, and repent in dust and ashes" (Job 42:3, 6). Their experiences opened their eyes to God's holiness.

Their sufferings were not penal; rather so that God could demonstrate His love in their circumstances. They experienced the hand of God because He loved them—not because He was angry or displeased with them.

Their outcome demonstrated God's mercy and grace. His servants emerged from their tests with greater love and trust for God. They learned to worship God just because He is *Elohim.* Just because He

60

is "*I AM*"—not because of what He did for them. They emerged knowing God through their own eyes no longer through the eyes of others.

They were no longer worshipping God at a distance. They were now coming into His presence with adoration, praise and thanksgiving for all things. Now they had an intimate relationship with God.

Joseph said, **"But God...."** Can you say, "but God," in your circumstances? I challenge you, "...choose you this day whom ye will serve..." (Joshua 24:15). Will it be God or man? If you choose to serve God, you must learn who God is through the principles in His Word.

If you choose to serve God, you must learn to live by God's standards. You must learn to receive God's love in the manner in which He chooses to express it.

If you determine to wait *in* the will of God and if you determine to *purpose in your heart* as Daniel did, you too will emerge saying, **"but God."** You too will emerge proclaiming, "*God meant it for my good.*"

CHAPTER FOUR

Why God Loves Me

"Yes, Jesus loves me!

Yes, Jesus loves me!

Yes, Jesus loves me!

The Bible tells me so."

When you look back over your life, you can trace your steps and see when you were living a life of submission and obedience or one of rebellion and disobedience.

You begin to ponder your actions and your attitudes, and you wonder why God would love a person like you. You can't count the number of times you have committed acts that were unkind, hateful and hurtful to others. In some instances, you have never repented of those acts, and you may feel you have a right to harbor your feelings.

There have been times that you have been so hardhearted that not even the love of God could penetrate your walls of defense you built up to *protect* your strongholds of fear, jealousy, suspicion, lack of forgiveness, self-indulgence, control and manipulation, wrong beliefs, wrong patterns of thinking and the list continues. You began filtering what you heard through a distorted belief system. These strongholds have convinced you there is no way God could love you.

In spite of all of your hang-ups and excuses, God loves you. Did you know that it is impossible for God to hate you? Although He does hate the sin you commit, God still loves the sinner because He loves His Son, Jesus Christ. Jesus gave His life for a ransom for sinners, and His blood covers the believer and makes him or her righteous (in right standing with God). So when God looks at you, He sees you through the blood of His Son, Jesus Christ, that covers your sin.

You may be thinking, *If that's the case, I may as well be what I want to be and do whatever I want to do because Jesus has got my back! After all, He paid the penalty for all of my sins.* You are right. Jesus paid the price for our sin. But He does not remove the consequences you will suffer when you sin.

The apostle Paul reminds us of our accountability when he asked the question in Romans 6:1, which says, "What shall we say then? Shall we continue in sin, that grace may abound?" He comes back in verse 2 with a firm response: "God forbid. How shall we, that are dead to sin, live any longer therein [in it]?"

What's wrong with you? Would you allow your lover and best friend to abuse you and think it was okay? I would think not. Well, neither does the lover of our soul, the Lord God almighty.

Christ loved the Father so much that He sought to do the will of the Father above all else. He came from heaven to earth to show us the way to the Father's heart. God made man in His image. Of all the creations God made, man is the only one that God chose to create in His image and likeness. God actually breathed His own breath into the nostrils of man and gave man life from His life. Genesis 2:7 says, *"And the* LORD *God formed man of the dust of the ground, and breathed into his nostrils the breath of life; and man became a living soul."* That image was shattered through sin and rebellion. But God said, "I still love My people, and I need a way to restore our relationship." So He sent His only Son, Jesus Christ, to die for you and me. Jesus became the propitiation for our sins. He took our place by sacrificing His life on the cross as a means of reconciling us to God, His Father.

In Bible days, a young man named Jeremiah sought to tell God's people why God loved them. His story begins in the book of Jeremiah chapter one. Jeremiah was a young priest and prophet of Anathoth, a prophet of great compassion. As a result of his compassion, he was nicknamed "*the weeping prophet.*" Jeremiah was committed to God and holiness. Jeremiah was anointed by God to deliver a message of warning and judgment and possible captivity to a small remnant of Judah who were his kinsmen. As a result, his own people persecuted him for proclaiming the truth of their impending captivity. This account is in Jeremiah chapters 19 and 20.

In spite of their rejection, Jeremiah never lost his love and compassion for the people. However, he did want to quit proclaiming God's Word when he said,

"For since I spoke, I cried out, I cried violence and spoil, because the word of the Lord was made a reproach unto me, and a derision, daily. Then I said, I will not make mention of him, nor speak any more in his name. But *his word* was in mine heart like a burning fire shut up in my bones, and I was weary with forbearing, and I could not refrain" (Jeremiah 20:8, 9).

The presence of God was so powerful in Jeremiah that God's love constrained his desire to quit or give up.

Prophecies had gone forth earlier by Jeremiah warning the families of the house of Israel that were living in Jerusalem to repent of their sins. He warned that if they refused to repent, their cities would be destroyed. As the story goes, the people of God refused to repent. Their cities were invaded by Nebuchadnezzar, the king of Babylon, and destroyed. The fall of Jerusalem was great.

Jeremiah is given a choice by King Nebuchadnezzar either to go to Babylon or to stay with the remnant of the poor who were left in Jerusalem. Jeremiah chose to stay in Jerusalem and minister to the remnant.

About seven months after their invasion and captivity, more trouble arose when Ishmael invaded the land. Some of the remnant in Jerusalem as well as the governor whom King Nebuchadnezzar had left in charge over Jerusalem were murdered. Now another portion of the remnant is carried away captive by Ishmael.

A man named Johanan stepped forward and planned a rescue effort; the portion of the remnant that had been taken away by Ishmael was recovered by Johanan and returned to the land.

Now Johanan and the entire remnant pursue Jeremiah to pray that God would show Jerusalem which way they should go as well as what they should do concerning their circumstances. Jeremiah received their petition and made intercession for them to the Lord. After ten days the Lord spoke to Jeremiah with *instruction* and *direction* for the people.

In chapter 29 God told Jeremiah that if the people would stay in the land in which they were dwelling (Jerusalem), He would build them and not pull them down. He would plant them and not pluck them up. He would even repent of the evil that He had done unto them. He included a word of exhortation for them not to be afraid of the king of Babylon because He was with them to save them and deliver them from the hand of the king. God said He would show them mercies and provide a way for them to return to their own land.

God further instructed Jeremiah saying, "If the people say they *will not* dwell in that land and *neither will we obey* the voice of the Lord, your God; but we will go into the land of Egypt" thinking that there they will find peace, food and prosperous living, then *destruction is their end.* God says what they feared most in the land of Jerusalem (the fear of dying by famine and pestilence) would surely overtake them in the land of Egypt if they chose to leave Jerusalem.

The people rejected the word of the Lord through Jeremiah and accused him of speaking falsely (people hate truth even when it's for their good). Through rejection and disobedience, the people began their descent to their own demise.

There are 52 chapters in the book of Jeremiah, and I have just taken you through the forty-third chapter to give you a general overview. Now let's return to Jeremiah chapter 4 and a few other books of the Bible to discover why God loves us.

Psalm 139:14 says, "I will praise thee; for I am fearfully and wonderfully made: marvelous are thy works, and that my soul knoweth right well."

Zechariah 2:8b declares, "for he that toucheth you toucheth the apple of his eye." Finally in Genesis 1:26, God said, "…Let us make man in our image, after our own likeness…."

The mystery of why God loves us begins to unfold in the preceding verses you have just read. As a result of being fearfully and wonderfully made, we are the apple of God's eye. *Therefore, captivity is inevitable!* That's the mystery most people don't understand. They don't understand why God would order captivity if we are the apple of His eye. *However, God said, "…whom I have caused to be carried away from Jerusalem into Babylon"* (Jeremiah 29:4). According to this verse, God will send us into captivity.

But oh, God *does* love us. *God loves us because He created us for the purpose of expressing His divine love in us and toward us. For God not to love His own image is impossible.*

God made man and gave man a moral nature with the ability to think, feel and have a will. Sometimes our will is in conflict with God's will for our lives. As a result, we, like the remnant of Judah, often find ourselves in conditions of captivity. Sometimes this captivity is self-imposed, and other times it is divinely appointed.

Verse 4 in chapter 29 holds the key: "Thus saith the LORD of hosts, the God of Israel, unto all that are carried away captives, *whom I have caused to be carried away from Jerusalem unto Babylon.*"

You do know that to be carried away in captivity does not always mean being displaced in the physical realm, don't you? You can be in captivity in your mind. I will take an even bolder stand and say in most cases this is where captivity begins and ends. Regardless of your condition of captivity, deliverance can only come by the Spirit. Keep this point in mind as you continue to read.

According to Ephesians 1:17, God desires that we have *"…the spirit of wisdom and revelation in the knowledge of him."* God reveals Himself according to His mighty names. His names represent His character, His deity and His acts. God declares who He is to His people. He presents His character based on their condition.

In Jeremiah 29:4, God refers to Himself as the *Lord of Host (Sabaoth).* This name gives reference to warfare or service. It is the name of the Lord in manifestation of power. It is a name related to heavenly bodies, angels, saints and sinners. *As Lord of Host,* God is able to marshal all these hosts to fulfill His purposes and to help His people. This name of God also reveals Him as *Jehovah-Nissi* who is the Lord my banner against conflict in the flesh. *Nissi* is the name of God that reveals God as the source of our victory in the flesh, and that victory is always wholly due to divine help from God.

It seems plausible that if our captivity is self-imposed, it is well deserved. However, the mystery remains and the struggle for most is to understand how a God of love, who created us in His image, would cause us to be carried away into seasons or places of captivity.

God says to Judah and to you *(insert your name here),* "I love you so much that *I will cause you to go through* a period of travail and captivity. I will purposely move you from a place of comfort where all your needs are met and separate you from your friends and family. Not only that, but I will *strategically* place you in a condition of bondage. I will disrupt your daily routines and your common places of fellowship."

What does God expect to accomplish in us through our period of captivity? *Well, I am glad you asked.* God wants to maximize your potential while you still have breath in your body. After all, no one can praise God from the grave. This is another example of God's revealing His character by His name. He is also named El-Shaddai. This is the name of God that manifests God as our strengthener and satisfier. Through this character God chastens His people unto greater fruit bearing. He accomplishes this by purifying us through purging. Babylon is a place of purging.

Purging is *not* a result of God's judgment or condemnation. It is a result of Genesis 1:23 wherein God declares He made us in His image. Therefore, when He looks at us and He does not see His image (His heavenly characteristics) in the reflection, He gets to work and *into captivity we go.*

In verse 5 the Lord speaks and tells the people that in their captivity they are to accomplish certain tasks. They are to build up the area so that it becomes a home for their families. They are to grow vegetation, plant gardens, eat of the produce that they grow, marry, produce children, and their children are to marry. Well, that sounds like a mighty long time that they will be in captivity.

According to verse 7 God says they are also to pray that the atmosphere in which they live will be peaceful. They are to seek opportunities to establish peace while in their new city. If they obey, there will be peace not only in their city but also in their mind. Did you know there could be peace all around you, and you still not experience the peace of God in your mind? Now that is true captivity! This is an important truth for you to receive at this point in your reading. God not only gives peace, God is peace. He is also known as Jehovah-Shalom. This name of God is the manifestation of God as "Peace." He will give you peace in your mind even when your circumstances and your condition say there is no peace.

Let's get back to the text. God warns the people in verses 8 and 9 not to entertain false prophecies because He has already given them a prophetic message over their lives and conditions. Therefore, there is no need to seek words from others who are unable to speak truth and protection over their own lives.

In verse ten God tells them the number of years they will be in captivity. He tells them their captivity will be seventy years. Throughout this period in exile, God will return and check out their stewardship and obedience.

God comes back at different intervals to see if they have completed the assignment He gave them. God does the same thing in our lives. He returns at unannounced intervals to check our stewardship, growth and obedience.

Then in the midst of their captivity, God writes the remnant a short love letter. In verse 11 God tells His people the lovely, wonderful thoughts He has toward them and that He has plans for their lives—to give them hope, prosperity and an expected end. So He takes time to encourage them and remind them of His great love and care for them and that this captivity has a divine purpose.

According to verses 12 through 14, when we stop having our pity party and begin to pray and seek the will of God (His plans and expected end), we discover not only His will, we find Him in the process. When we find God, we find life. "For whoso findeth me findeth life, and shall obtain favor of the LORD" (Proverbs 8:35). God declares then He will hear and respond to our prayers. He will gather us back to Himself from these strange places of captivity and bondage. God says that *He will be found by us.* As we already discovered in Ephesians 1:17, His ultimate goal for mankind is that Jesus gives us the spirit of wisdom and revelation in the knowledge of God. In other words God wants us to know Him through the revelation the Holy Spirit will give.

I believe that some of you who are reading this book are in Babylon. You are in a *tight place*, a *place of captivity and bondage*, and you have been there a long time. You have not accepted your Babylonian experience in the spirit of God, and you have not sought God's face. You have been living a life of grumbling, running and complaining.

The only progress you have experienced in your captivity is that you have now moved to a level of complacency, and you no longer want to leave Babylon. *But Babylon is not your home*; Jerusalem is your home! God never intended for you to remain and die in Babylon. You are just passing through.

So you ask, where is Jerusalem? Jerusalem is in the will of God. It is the presence of God. Jerusalem is a spiritual sphere or realm in which we operate on earth until we reach that heavenly city of Jerusalem. God dwells in Jerusalem—that heavenly city not made with hands. It is a dwelling place for the saints of God. Abraham looked for that city, *"For he looked for a city which hath foundations, whose builder and maker is God"* (Hebrews 11:10). *"But now they desire a better country, that is, an heavenly: wherefore God is not ashamed to be called their God: for he hath prepared for them a city"* (Hebrew 11:16).

God never intended for you to get comfortable with your dwelling place on earth. When you begin to get too comfortable, God will cause you to go into Babylon. He desires that you are forever looking for greater opportunity to get where He is. Until we get to heaven, the only way we are able to get where He is, is through worship.

God is a Spirit, and we worship Him in spirit and in truth. Since you are made in the *image of God,* no matter what you experience in the physical, you will have to learn to handle all of your circumstances through the Spirit of God that dwelleth *in you.* Because God is a Spirit, He can only respond to you through His Spirit that lives in you. You will never find peace, hope, joy, power, restoration and deliverance (salvation) in any other person or thing. *It can only be found in God.*

Jesus Christ, born of virgin Mary, came to earth for a short while. *Why?* It was brief because God never intended for Christ to remain on earth (Christ's Babylon experience). He was just passing through.

Christ is our example. Christ was to experience and suffer that which God had appointed over His life. Remember, it is God's plans and expected end—not *your* plans and *your* expected end. Jesus was to accomplish the task God gave Him.

Jesus was to glorify His Father in and through His captivity experience. He was to see the glory (the purpose of God fulfilled) in His suffering.

He was to die to self and rise unto the Father to complete the will of God. In His new spiritual body, Jesus would accomplish even greater work—greater fruit bearing by ministering unto the throne of God by bringing redemption and salvation to mankind.

That's all God wants out of your Babylonian experiences. God loves you, and He wants your life to glorify Him. God wants you to learn to glorify Him *in* your sufferings. Die to self. Rise to the Father in your spirit and minister to God through your life.

That's why God loves you. He gave His only Son that you might have a right to life through salvation. God created you in His image. *God cannot hate Himself.* God loves you because He loves His presence that lives inside you. Remember, when God breathed His breath into your nostrils, He breathed His Spirit into your physical body. God desires to bless you to walk into your destiny. Receive God's loves for your life and begin to experience a loving relationship with God; this relationship compares to none you will ever know.

God bless you, *God loves you.*

CHAPTER 5

IT'S A GOOD THING

One of Gods truth's is that it is a good thing that we suffer in the will of God. Why is it a good thing that we suffer? Because it produces Godly character in us, and if we want to experience God, we must suffer as Christ suffered. Suffering is also one of those inherited benefits. However, we do not have to earn this benefit.

Trust me, this *one* is freely given. As a matter of fact, it comes upon you whether or not you like it and when you least expect it. Did you know that it's a good thing that we suffer in the will of God? Remember when I used that phrase "great *Guglamuuglia"* in chapter three? Well, it fits here also. I referred you to Isaiah 30:20, which says, *"And though the Lord give you the bread of adversity, and the water of affliction, yet shall not thy teachers be removed into a corner any more, but thine eyes shall see thy teachers."*

Revisiting that text at this point in the book is important because the course of your thinking must change in order for you to receive what the Holy Spirit has to say in the remaining chapters.

In this fifth chapter, you will need to make the decision to alter the course of your destiny by making a paradigm shift in your thinking and begin to walk into the destiny that God has for you. I say that because the way you view your circumstances, conditions and experiences from this point on is literally a matter of life and death. Living is more than breathing. Did you know you could be breathing and still not have life? Therefore, life is more than the act of breathing in oxygen and expelling carbon monoxide.

Jesus said that He came that we might have life and that we might have it more abundantly. Therefore, I am inclined to believe that He knew more than we do about life. His comments would suggest that although you are living, you might in fact not have life. This is what is known as one of those hard sayings of Christ. This saying is hard because it is difficult for man to understand a spiritual saying when he attempts to comprehend God through human intellect. So to that man the things of God become a mystery. *Mysteries* are "hidden spiritual truths that God reveals to those who are prepared to receive the truth of His Word in the Spirit."

I have already stated that strongholds are spiritual forces such as anger, envy, jealousy that dominate or occupy areas of the mind that reinforce our belief system. We channel what we hear and see through these belief systems. If those belief systems are distorted, we will in turn distort the *truth* when it is presented to us. As a result, we live our lives based on damaged feeling and emotions. We live what is commonly known today as *dysfunctional* lives. Remember, I have already stated that positions with God do not entitle us to all of God's benefits.

God reserves communicating His truths to those who do not channel His Holy Word through damaged emotions and distorted belief systems. The fact that God chooses to whom He will communicate His truths is an important principle for the believer to accept and understand. God determines when and to whom He will bestow His benefits. Some benefits are given because of our relationship to God as the Father.

Romans 1:16 says, "For I am not ashamed of the gospel of Christ: for it is the power of God unto salvation to everyone that believeth.... Romans 10:9 says, "That if thou shalt confess with thy mouth the Lord Jesus, and shalt believe in thine heart that God hath raised him from the dead, thou shalt be saved." The benefit is salvation; the prerequisite is confession. The benefit is the provision of God to perform the transformation in you and give you eternal life. It becomes a benefit that you have not worked to earn. You simply inherit the benefit of eternal life through salvation. It is a benefit solely because of your relationship to God as His redeemed son or daughter.

There are other benefits that must be earned. One benefit you must earn is having the knowledge and understanding of God's truths. Let me explain what I mean. II Timothy 2:15 says, "Study to shew [show] thyself approved unto God, a workman that needeth not to be ashamed, rightly dividing the word of truth." Several key words in this text support my previous comments. They are "study," "show ourselves," and "approved unto God." God says we must meet several prerequisites in order to understand His truths.

The first prerequisite to gaining understanding is that we must study. To *study* means "to learn, research or to examine closely in pursuit of knowledge." To have *knowledge* means "to gain an understanding." Having knowledge of a process, concept or a person teaches you how to take that understanding and make sound judgments. As a result of having an understanding in the application of what you have learned, you now have the ability to apply the knowledge acquired to conduct your daily affairs.

The second requirement was that we had to show ourselves. Our experiences in life will eventually reveal what we are made of. Our experiences reveal what's on the inside of us—our motives, our nature, our purpose and the intent of our heart. This *showing ourselves* may be referred to as our "proving or testing ground." We prove our worth to God through testing. II Timothy 2:20 says the following:

"But in a great house there are not only vessels of gold and of silver, but also of wood and earth; *and some to honor*, and some to dishonor. If a man therefore purge himself from these, he shall be a vessel unto honour, sanctified, and meet [fit; one that meets the requirement] for the master's use, and prepared unto every good work."

We are an investment to God. Showing ourselves through testing allows God to determine when and or if we are ready to become vessels of honor that God can make a deposit of His biblical truths.

This revelation of who we are is not only revealed to others around us but to ourselves as well. You see God already knows us; His objective is to get us to see ourselves through His eyes. Unless we become real and honest with ourselves about our weaknesses, faults and shortcomings, God cannot use us at our maximum potential.

God is a refiner. Malachi 3:2 and 3 says, "But who may abide the day of his coming? and who shall stand when he appeareth? For he is like a refiner's fire, and like fullers' soap. And he shall sit like a refiner and a purifier of silver...." God has every intention of helping you see what He sees in you. Now that thought can be quite frightening!

Refiners purify their objects with heat—*lots of heat!* That's exactly what God does. He turns up the heat and sticks us in the fire in order to burn off the residue of anger, shame, low self-esteem, bitterness, resentment, rebellion, lack of forgiveness, hurt, and anything else left as a result of bad relationships and experiences. Sometimes it seems like we have already suffered enough, and God allows or sends us through more suffering experiences. God knows what it takes to bring us forth as pure gold. Remember? I said that when God looks at us and does not see His reflection, into the fire we go!

The third requirement that must be met before God will reveal His truth to us is that we must be *approved unto God* for ministry work. The life of Job was addressed in chapter three. Only after God had tested Job through much suffering was he *acceptable* to and *approved* of by God. Job 42:8 says, "...and my servant Job shall pray for you: *for him will I accept...*" You too want to be acceptable to God so that God will receive your prayers as He received Job's prayers. God would not receive the prayers of Job's three friends because they were not purified and approved unto God.

In the New Testament, Paul admonishes Christians in the same light when he says, "I beseech you therefore, brethren, by the mercies of God, that ye present your bodies a living sacrifice, holy, acceptable unto God, which is your reasonable service." We must be made acceptable to God through the Refiner's purification fire before God will reveal His truth to us. Remember the revelation of His truth is a revelation of who God is. God will not reveal Himself in intimate ways to strangers.

Now let's put all three requirements together so that we can see how we meet God's prerequisite. In the gospel of Matthew 11:29, Jesus said, "Take my yoke upon you, and learn of me...." What was Jesus saying? Jesus was saying, "Take on My likeness or My ways by examining or observing the things that I say and do." Jesus said, "Observe My humility, sacrifice, conversation, obedience, patience and My servanthood; that's the yoke that I want you take upon yourselves."

Jesus knew we had the ability to take on His likeness if we studied His ways. He knew this was the only way we would meet God's prerequisite. He knew we would have to earn the benefit of having God's truth revealed to us, so we can begin to understand the mysteries of God. He knew this inherited benefit would only come after much testing and *suffering* at the hand of God. Only then could we be approved to God as a worthy vessel of honor.

God uses vessels of honor that He can trust to communicate His truths. These vessels are able to communicate the Word of God as God intended it to be taught. That Word must be uncompromised—even when it feels like you are perceived as a prophet of doom.

Romans 8:17 says, "And if children, then heirs; heirs of God, and joint heirs with Christ; if so be that we suffer with him, that we may be also glorified together." I Peter 2:20 says, "For what glory is it if, when ye are buffeted for your faults, ye shall take it patiently? but if, when ye do well, and suffer for it, ye take it patiently, *this is acceptable to God.*"

The character of God was addressed at length in chapter four. God is more concerned about your character than your reputation; therefore, He does whatever it takes to get your attention. God is interested in developing your character into *godly* character. That's why Jesus invites us to take His yoke (likeness) upon us. The suffering is *good* when it is in the will of God—whether it be sent or allowed. Romans 8:28 says, *"And we know that all things work together for the good to them that love God, to them who are the called according to his purpose."* People often misquote this verse by omitting several important portions of the Scripture. The verse gives several conditions that must be met in order to receive the inheritance by which our circumstances will always be considered *good*.

First, the promise is based on whether or not we love God. Paul, the writer of the text, reaffirms the commandment that Jesus gave in Luke 10:27 that we are to "...love the Lord our God with all of our heart, and with all of our soul, and with all our strength, and with all of our mind...." So Paul's first contingency to inheriting the promise was based on our love for God.

Secondly, Paul says the promise is only applicable to certain candidates. Having all circumstances work out for good is restricted to those candidates who live in the will and purpose of God and to those who are "the called according to His purpose." These requirements mean even though we evaluate our experiences based on what we see, taste, hear, smell and touch, we must learn to look for the spiritual meaning in all our experiences. Remember? This point was emphasized through the Babylonian experience.

The believer's first response should be to run into His presence. When getting in His presence becomes as natural to us as breathing air, then we know we have experienced growth and development.

It is a good thing that we suffer in the will of God when our mind tells us there are *no other options* and without Him we die. The mere thought of living without Him frightens us so much that we repent from even thinking such a horrible thought. You may feel like this truth is some great secret or hidden mystery that few people find. I believe that conjecture is true. Perhaps you still feel that the manifestation of God's love toward you through your suffering could not possibly be a good thing.

Let's look at the Scripture to see what God has to say about the issue. Although God desires that all men be saved, He knows that not all men desire life eternal. In Matthew 7:13 and 14 and the first several Psalms, the Bible says that there are fundamentally only two lifestyles and there are, in essence, only two ways a man can live his life.

Matthew 7 13, 14, "Enter ye in at the strait gate: for wide is the gate, and broad is the way, that leadeth to destruction, and many there be who go in that way. Because strait is the gate, and narrow is the way, which leadeth unto life, and few there be that find it."

What did Jesus mean? He was telling the disciples that when people start out on the journey of life, they find all types of attractions and distractions. Jesus knew many people would find growing wealthy in the possessions of this world more attractive than growing wealthy in the Spirit.

Jesus knew we would yield to enticements that would gratify our flesh. He knew many would take the path of death and destruction rather than the path leading to life and victory. Choosing the path of life means people will have to choose Christ. In John 14:6, Jesus said, "…I am the way, the truth, and the life…." He knew very few would find the *strait way*—let alone enter into the *narrow gate*.

Entering into the strait gate requires *discipline, obedience* and *faithfulness* to God's biblical principles and precepts. It requires precision to stay on the path that leads to the strait gate.

These verses compare and contrast two ways of life. People are either on the road that leads to life or they are traveling on the road that leads to destruction. That many people have no idea that they are on the road to destruction is remarkable. They get up day after day, perform their routines, attain their personal objectives and goals for the day, and lie down each night with a sense of pride and admiration for their accomplishments and successes.

Is it wrong to be prosperous, successful and established in the eyes of man? No. In fact, God desires exactly that for those who obey Him.

Joshua 1:8 says, "This book of the law shall not depart out of thy mouth; but thou shalt meditate therein day and night, that thou mayest observe to do according to all that is written therein; for then thou shalt make thy way prosperous, and then thou shalt have good success."

Proverbs 10:22 says, "The blessing of the LORD, it maketh rich, and he addeth no sorrow with it." *Yes,* God desires that you be rich, and He says that when He makes you rich, there is no sorrow or problems that come along with the increase. If I still sound like I am contradicting myself, let's take a closer look at Matthew 7:13 and 14 to see what Jesus meant.

The first lifestyle contrasts a lifestyle that seems to have no boundaries or rules for living. It would appear that you do not have to be disciplined or have much structure in your life to travel along this road.

Based on that premise, it is likely you will often get lost and find yourself going in the wrong direction. Jesus says, "This gate is *wide* and *broad is the way."* Notice He does not provide any detours for those on this road. The end for those on this road is destruction.

Jesus predicts that those who travel down this road will have many friends to keep them company. How do I know that? Because Jesus said the gate that leads to destruction is wide. The gate is wider to allow passage for the large crowd that will go through.

Who are these people about whom Jesus is speaking? In this text He was speaking of those who have riches. I know I just struck a chord with some of you, and you are ready to slap the covers of this book together and throw it against a wall. Before you do that, please let me explain.

In Mark 10:17 through 27, Jesus explains His position to the disciples. The text addresses a rich young ruler seeking eternal life. Jesus acknowledges to the young man that clearly he knows all of the commandments, but apparently, he lacks one important characteristic. It seems that this rich young ruler had placed all his heart in his wealth and ability to accumulate great fortune. His treasure is in his pocket; yet he makes no investment in his future governing his heart and eternal life. Jesus recognized and noted that it would be difficult for the rich to enter into the kingdom of God.

The kingdom of God is the place of salvation that is only entered into by way of the new birth. When we seek the kingdom of God, we are saying we want God's sovereign rule exercised in the earth as it is exercised in heaven. What you may not have realized was God's will is done on earth as it is done in heaven through vessels who do the will of the Father.

Jesus knew that for some, a vast accumulation of riches would be a distraction and wealth would become their stronghold. Some would feel life without wealth would not be worth living. Some may not feel the need for Christ in their life because their salvation is in their wealth, and God would not have authority over their lives.

I am not picking on the rich. After all, God is rich in houses and land and owns all the cattle on a thousand hills. God created all that is royal. As a matter of fact, the book of Revelation says, that great city of heaven—the holy Jerusalem—has a wall made of jasper, and the city is pure gold. So rich in splendor is the city that the foundations of the wall of the city are garnished with all manner of precious stones such as jasper, sapphire, chalcedony, emerald, sardonyx, sardius, chrysolite, beryl, topaz, chrysoprasus, jacinth and amethyst. The chapter further describes the beauty of the city's having gates made of pearl, and that the street of that city was pure gold (Revelation 21). No matter how much wealth you have accumulated on earth, it does not begin to compare to God's riches in heaven. *So* just hold on a minute and keep reading!

This narrow road and a strait gate have been addressed. What do you need to do to gain admittance through the strait gate? Well, it means you will have to pack your bags in preparation for travel on the narrow (difficult) road of life. It means your paradigm shift would have to have occurred. *Well, how do I do that?* you may be wondering. *And if it is a difficult road to travel, why would I want to pick that road over the easier road?* Well, I'm glad you asked. The first thing you have to do is determine if you are righteous or ungodly. I know I just lost a few of you right here! *But don't close this book!*

According to the first few Psalms, there are also two types of people in life—the righteous and the ungodly. God compares the ungodly to the sinner. He says the *righteous man* is "the man who finds delight in keeping the law (Biblical principles to live by) of the Lord." As a matter of fact, the righteous man enjoys keeping his thoughts day and night on Biblical principles. This man finds greater delight in meditating on God's Word and keeping God's commandments than in being entertained by man or pleasing man.

Few will find delight in meditating and accepting the Word of God because it requires great sacrifice and obedience. When we meditate on God's Word, we provide the Holy Spirit sufficient time to speak to us and tell us what God has to say about His Word as it applies to our situation. Once a truth becomes a revelation to us and the eyes of our understanding have been opened, we are held accountable for that knowledge. The liberation occurs in the acquisition of knowledge, understanding and accepting the truth. John 8:32 says, "And ye shall know the truth, and the truth shall make you free." When we decide to accept the truth, we can experience freedom like never before. We will no longer quench what God has put in us as natural hunger because we have learned that He alone can satisfy that hunger.

The fight is over, and life begins. What is most strange about this spiritual awakening is that many people don't actually begin to live until it's almost time for them to die. They wasted their time seeking the pleasures of this world as a means of satisfying their hunger and thirst. That form of slow death is in itself a means of suffering.

This type of suffering apart from God is not a good thing! Consequently, this type of suffering results in self-destruction because the person is living outside of the will of God. That unquenchable thirst is what initiated their search for fulfillment that took them to places they should not have gone. That search for fulfillment took longer than they realized it would take. The person becomes lost and confused. This is a thirst that can only be quenched in the presence of God. David said in Psalm 42:1, "As the hart [deer] panteth after the water brooks, so panteth [longeth] my soul after thee...." He had learned that the source of life was in his soul where God dwells. When a man fails to meet the longing of his soul, death is imminent. My friend, *this* is a suffering death that is experienced while you are still breathing and going about your daily routine.

The suffering of the saint that has been tested, tried and proven by the Refiner's fire results in joy. James 1:2 and 2 says, "My brethren, count it all joy when ye fall into various temptations [trials; test]. Knowing this, that the testing of your faith worketh patience." Remember, patience was one of the virtues that Christ possesses and one that we should possess as we work to take on His likeness. Patience is another benefit; however, this one must be earned. And patience is not earned without great sacrifice.

It's a good thing that we suffer—*when we suffer in the will of God*. It's a good thing that we suffer—*when we learn to praise God in the midst of our suffering*. It's a good thing that we suffer—*when it brings us to the point of recognition that our soul cannot survive apart from God's indwelling presence*. It's a good thing that we suffer—*when we learn to count it all joy*.

Paul said in Philippians 4:11–13:

"Not that I speak in respect of want or need: for I have *learned*, in whatever state I am, therewith to be content. I know both how to be abased, and I *know* how to abound: everywhere and in all things I am instructed both to be full and to be hungry, both to abound and *to suffer* need. I can do all things through Christ which strengtheneth me."

Paul did not say this simply to create a popular *cliché*. He was able to say this truth because it was *the truth*. Paul had learned he really could do all things through Christ who gave him strength. He said it as a result of having passed through the Refiner's fire. Acts 14:19 says, "And there came thither certain Jews from Antioch and Iconium, who persuaded the people, and having stoned Paul, drew him out of the city, supposing he had been dead."

"…they caught Paul and Silas… And brought them to the magistrates… And the multitude rose up together against them… And when they had laid many stripes upon them, they cast them into the inner prison, and made their feet fast in the stocks" (Acts 16:19–24).

Acts 23:12 and 13 says, "And when it was day, certain of the Jews banded together, and bound themselves under a curse, saying that they would neither eat nor drink till they had killed Paul. And they were more than forty who had made this conspiracy."

Paul was no stranger to persecution, pain and suffering, and some of you who are reading this book are no strangers to persecution, pain and suffering. As we have learned through Christ, suffering is an inherited benefit from God. Paul summarizes his experiences with God in II Corinthians 11:24–27 by saying:

"Of the Jews five times received I forty *stripes* save one. Thrice was I beaten with rods, once was I stoned, thrice I suffered shipwreck, a night and a day I have been in the deep; *In* journeyings often, *in* perils of waters, *in* perils of robbers, *in* perils by *mine own* countrymen, *in* perils by the heathen, *in* perils in the city, *in* perils in the wilderness, *in* perils in the sea, *in* perils among false brethren; In weariness and painfulness, in watchings often, in hunger and thirst, in fastings often, in cold and nakedness."

In Acts 20:24, Paul makes a rich farewell statement saying, "*But none of these things move me,* neither count I my life dear unto myself, so that I might finish my course with *joy*…." Paul was not disheartened by his sufferings; rather, he loved God all the more.

If you would turn to the Father in the midst of your pain with a contrite heart, God will receive you. God is ready to extend His love and comfort to you this very instant. Along with Paul, you too will need to make a declaration of your love to the Father. God is waiting on you to come to Him.

In Isaiah 28:5 and 6, the prophet Isaiah says,

"In *that* day shall the LORD of host be for a crown of glory, and for a diadem of beauty, unto the residue of his people, And for a spirit of justice to him that sitteth in judgment, and for strength to those who turn the battle to the gate."

A *diadem* is "a crown or a headband worn as a sign of royalty and power." Just imagine, the blessing from suffering in the will of God is a crown that represents God's anointing power in your life. In verse 12 Isaiah says, "To whom he said, This is the *rest* wherewith ye may cause the weary to rest; and this is the refreshing: yet they would not hear." Isaiah follows up this verse in chapter 30 by saying, "For thus saith the Lord GOD, the Holy One of Israel; In returning and *rest* shall ye be saved; in quietness and in confidence shall be your strength; and ye would not" (v. 15).

Notice Isaiah ends verses 12 and 15 with a heartbreaking statement: *"...yet they would not hear"* and *"...and ye would not"*. In both verses, the people rejected God's love and God's ways. They rejected God's inheritance. Their rest, strength, refreshment and salvation were in their *coming* to God through their suffering experiences. So as it was with Paul, so it is with you.

You have grown weary and desire rest, yet you refuse to come to God. You have grown cold and distant in your heart, yet you refuse to return to God. "But ye said, 'No,' and you continue to flee from God instead of running into His arms."

In **that** day-**your** *day of pain*-when you come and return to God, He will be that crown of glory, a diadem of beauty, a spirit of justice and strength to you who turn the battle to the gate. Cry out to the Father and fall upon Him. He will take you in His loving arms, caress your soul and restore your joy.

Through your pain, heartache and confusion...*come*. God's grace is there to comfort you. His mercy is there to save you, and you too, as did Paul, will declare...*it's a good thing.*

Father, I thank You for teaching me to see my experiences, life, relationships, inheritance, nature and even my sufferings through *your* eyes and not through my emotions.

Amen.

CHAPTER SIX

I WILL BLESS YOU AT ALL TIMES

There are actually two perspectives to this statement: "I will bless you at all times." One perspective is *from man to God.* The other perspective is *from God to man.* Let's look at the perspective from man to God first. Psalm 34:1 says, "*I will bless the LORD at all times:* his praise shall continually be in my mouth."

David began the thirty-fourth Psalm with a vow to bless God—no matter what occurred in his life. What you don't see in this verse is what David had experienced prior to making that declaration. If you go back and begin with the first Psalm, you will find that by the time you reach the thirty-fourth, David has lived through mountaintop experiences as well as death-valley experiences. Taking a journey back through the books of I and II Samuel and I and II Chronicles to review this account of David's experiences will show how and why he is able to make this profound declaration.

First, it is good to know David. As a young man, David lived in Bethlehem with his brothers and his father Jesse. God anointed David king of Israel while he was in his early teens; however, it was many years thereafter that he would actually take the throne. A king whose name was Saul was already presiding over Israel. In I Samuel chapters 8–10, God used the prophet Samuel to anoint Saul as king of Israel. By chapter 16 of I Samuel, Saul's incomplete obedience to God had cost him his kingship. God rejected Saul from being king because he sinned and transgressed the commandment and the Word of the

Lord. King Saul was more concerned about what the people would say about him than the commandment of God, so he obeyed the dictates of the people.

"And Samuel said [to King Saul], Hath the LORD as great delight in burnt offerings and sacrifices, as in obeying the voice of the LORD? Behold, to obey is better than sacrifice, and to hearketh than the fat of rams. For rebellion is as the sin of witchcraft, and stubbornness is as iniquity and idolatry. Because thou hast rejected the word of the LORD, he hath also rejected thee from being king" (I Samuel 15:22, 23).

And Saul replied to Samuel:

"...I have sinned: for I have transgressed the commandment of the LORD, and thy words: because I feared the people, and obeyed their voice. Now therefore, I pray thee, pardon my sin, and turn again with me, that I may worship the LORD. And Samuel said unto Saul, I will not return with thee: for thou hast rejected the word of the LORD, and the LORD hath rejected thee from being king over Israel. And as Samuel turned about to go away, he [Saul] laid hold upon the skirt of his mantle, and it rent [tore]. And Samuel said unto him, The LORD hath rent the kingdom of Israel from thee this day, and hath given it to a neighbor of thine, that is better than thou" (I Samuel 15:24-28).

God had given King Saul specific instructions in how he was to destroy the Amalekites, but Saul chose to ignore God's instruction. As a result, the Lord used the prophet Samuel to communicate His displeasure to King Saul and His regret that He had made Saul the king of Israel. Samuel told King Saul in verse 19 that his disobedience was evil in the sight of the Lord.

King Saul tried to justify his actions in verse 20, saying he in fact did obey the voice of God and blamed the error on the people. He told Samuel that the spoil they had acquired from raiding the Amalekites was a good thing because they had made it a sacrificial offering to God.

Samuel rebuked King Saul, as if to say, "Do you think God would honor the wealth or possession you have obtained by dishonoring His word? Do you really think God would be pleased with the offering you have acquired by your own selfish means? How dare you think God would receive such a tainted offering! Your rebellion is just as appalling as if you had participated in an act of witchcraft."

God was saying, "Your stubborn ways have come up before Me, and I see that as iniquity and a form of idolatry. Samuel said, "Therefore, as you have chosen to reject the word from the Lord, the Lord will now reject you and remove you from your position of leadership as king of Israel."

So God gave instruction to Samuel to anoint a new king, and that king would be Saul's neighbor, David. I Samuel chapter 16 provide an account of David's ordination.

Samuel visited David's home and visually inspected Jesse's sons to select the new king from among them. Samuel was sure the new king was Jesse's son, Eliab, with his handsome features, his great physical strength and his significant stature. However, God had given Samuel specific instructions in verse 7 about what qualities to look for in the future king.

"But the LORD said unto Samuel, Look not on the countenance, or on the height of his stature; because I have refused him: for the LORD seeth not as man seeth; for man looketh on the outward appearance, but the LORD looketh on the heart."

The Lord told Samuel that none of the sons he had seen had fit God's criteria. Samuel said, *"...The LORD hath not chosen these."* So he asked Jesse, "Are all your children here?"

When Jesse replied that the youngest son was out in the pastures keeping the sheep, Samuel said, "...Send and fetch him: for we *will not* sit down till he come hither" (I Samuel 16:11).

"And he sent, and brought him in. Now he was ruddy, and withal of a beautiful countenance, and goodly [handsome] to look to. And the

LORD said, Arise, anoint him: *for this is he.* Then Samuel took the horn of oil, and anointed him in the midst of his brethren: and the Spirit of the LORD came upon David from that day forward" (vv. 12, 13).

Notice David was not Samuel's first choice, but he was God's first choice. After all this was done, David simply returned to the pasture and resumed his daily routine of taking care of sheep.

Remember I have already mentioned that God does what He wants to do when He wants to and with whomever He chooses? Notice David was out in the field minding his own business. He had gone to work like any other day, tending the sheep, getting dirty and smelly.

He did his job in the heat, cold and the rain. Then all of a sudden one day, a man came to his house unannounced. Lo and behold, David was summoned from his daily routine by what appeared to be a common man. But he was really summoned to leave his job and come home by God through God's prophet, Samuel.

What does the Bible reveal about David's personality? The Bible describes David as having a beautiful countenance, and he was handsome. The word *beautiful* means "proper, goodly." Its highest form applies to that which appeals to the senses or the mind. *Beautiful* also means "that which stirs a heightened response of the senses and of the mind on its highest level." Notice God did not ascribe the word *lovely* as a description of David because lovely rouses emotion rather than intellectual appreciation. Nor did the text say he was *pretty*, which suggests "appeal based on one's feelings," and those feelings are typically of a limited and superficial nature. However, the text *does* say David was *handsome*, which suggests "visual appeal based on conformity to ideals of form from another's view." David is also described as *ruddy*, which, according to the *American Heritage Dictionary*, means "glowing and healthy appearance, reddish or flushed."

We can see God selected a king with great intellectual strength and ability—one who was physically healthy and fair to look upon in physical appearance that would appeal to others and win their respect and favor.

In I Samuel 16:14, the Bible noted that the Spirit of the Lord departed from Saul, and an evil spirit from the Lord now troubled him. So Saul's servant recommended to Saul that he have a skillful player on the harp play for him whenever this evil spirit comes upon him. The playing of the harp will sooth Saul and relieve him from the evil spirit.

When David's name was put before King Saul, the king sent for David to come into his court. David played skillfully and majestically before King Saul. As a result, David found favor and was greatly loved by Saul. Consequently, Saul asked Jesse, David's father, to let David stay with him and become the king's armor bearer. When David played the harp, the evil spirit departed from Saul, and he was refreshed and made well. So Jesse gave David permission to live in the palace with King Saul.

All seemed to be going well for David. He was living in the palace as the king's armor bearer. He had a great anointing over his life to be king, and yet no move had been made to put him in position as king.

It was as if God had stalled the installation of his kingship. *Why?* God knew David was not ready for the job. *Yes,* he was the man for the job, but he was not yet equipped to perform the job. God knew what lay ahead for David. God knew He would have to take David through mountaintop and death-valley experiences to produce the heart of a worshipper in David—a heart that would bless God at all times.

Yes, you have been given a prophetic word. God has sent a prophet to anoint your head with oil. God has anointed you in the spirit, but you're still not ready for the ministry which God has given you. It matters not that you are old in age; *you're still young in your mind.* You have not learned that it is better to obey the voice of God rather than the voice of the people. You have not learned God is not interested nor is He impressed with your sacrifices. God is only interested and impressed with your obedience. So God has stalled your installation into the ministry which He has given you. Even though you have been chosen by God, He still reserves the right to determine when He will say, *"Arise, now is the time."*

God now began to take David through a series of experiences that lasted a lifetime. Seriously, I mean *a lifetime*. You see, an anointing from God is a grave responsibility, and it requires a lifetime commitment. It's not about being up front and winning the approval of others. It's all about fulfilling the will of God in and through you. That's what Jesus meant when He prayed, *"Thy kingdom come. Thy will be done in earth, as it is in heaven"* (Matthew 6:10).

The kingdom is God's divine purpose accomplished in and through the life of man. It is fulfilling God's will here in the earth, through man's daily routine. It doesn't just mystically and mysteriously happen; God plans it. God selects individuals He can trust to accomplish His divine purpose and fulfill His will through their lives. In earlier chapters we said these vessels had to be vessels of honor—vessels that are able to take God's truths and communicate them to God's people as God intended. The vessel cannot take the Word of God and filter it through distorted ways of thinking as Saul did in an attempt to justify wrong actions.

David's experiences began his long journey of *sorting through God's love*. He had no idea he would be taking the journey. He had no idea what to expect once he discovered it was, in fact, a journey. He had not asked for the position and title of *king*. It happened because he had the potential for God to maximize his talents and gifts for God's glory. Even at an early age, he had a love for God and was obedient to God's Word. He had a maturity that surpassed the understanding and obedience of most men twice his age.

How do I know this? Look at I Samuel chapter 17. Goliath of Gath, a Philistine of great stature, stood six cubits and a span. He wore a helmet of bronze and a coat that weighed five thousand shekels. Goliath defied the armies of Israel and challenged them to a fight.

After many days of battle between the Philistine army and the army of God, Goliath appeared. When the army of Israel saw Goliath, they were filled with fear and fled from the battle. Then up stepped a ruddy-faced little lad named David, whose anger was kindled as he heard Goliath's jeers.

"And David left his baggage in the hand of the keeper of the baggage, and ran into the army, and came and saluted [greeted] his brethren. And as he talked with them, behold, there came up the champion, the Philistine of Gath, Goliath by name, out of the armies of the Philistines, *and spake according to the same words:* and David heard *them*" (vv. 22, 23).

In verse 32 David responded, "…Let no man's heart fail because of him: thy servant will go and fight with this Philistine." David told Saul that he had killed both a lion and a bear with his bare hands, and as far as he is concerned, Goliath would be likened to that bear or lion, seeing he had defied the armies of the living God.

David refused to let any man, or any beast make a mockery of his God and/or the people of God. He had committed his life to blessing God at all times. So David prepared for battle with the giant, Goliath. David knew he served Jehovah Elohim, and he was willing to fight and even die for his strong conviction and *love for God.* But David surprised everyone when he refused to fight with the conventional weapons of his day. Instead, he said to Goliath:

"…Thou comest to me with a sword, and with a spear, and with a shield; but I come to thee in the name of the LORD of hosts, the God of the armies of Israel, whom though hast defied. This day will the LORD deliver thee into mine hand; and I will smite thee, and take thine head from thee; and I will give the carcasses of the host of the Philistines this day unto the fowls of the air, and to the wild beasts of the earth; that all the earth may know that there is a God in Israel. And all this assembly shall know that the LORD saveth not with the sword and spear; for the battle is the LORD's, and he will give you into our hands" (vv. 45-47).

Chapter one addressed the various names of God. David called upon God by the name of the *Lord of Hosts or Jehovah Sabaoth.* This name of God gives special reference to warfare or service. It is the name of God in manifestation of power. As the Lord of Hosts, God is able to marshal angels, sinners, saints, and heavenly bodies to fulfill His purposes and to help His people. David was not concerned about the battle because the *Lord of Hosts* was his God.

David began his journey of *sorting through God's love* in battle. God did not tell us in advance what our path will be to discover the ways in which He manifests His love for us, toward us and in us. God is not obligated to tell us all that is involved in the anointing He gives. *That's part of the sorting process.* God did not warn David that He would *discipline him through the delay* of his installation as king. God does not explain why He chooses the discipline of delay to teach us how to persevere in the face of opposition, suffering and peril, but He does prepare us by equipping us with spiritual gifts.

God gifted David with the mind of a warrior. Little did David know that he not only had an anointing to carry the title of *king*, but he was also given an anointing to fight wars in physical confrontation that could only be won through the spiritual intervention of God. Did he ask God to make him a fighter? No. Did he want to fight all of his days? Probably not, but he was *willing* because the love he had for God was greater than the love he had for life. *David had a desire to bless God at all times—even at an early age.*

The fight begins, and *God is with David.*

"And it came to pass, when the Philistine arose, and came, and drew near to meet David, that David hastened, and ran toward the army to meet the Philistine. And David put his hand in his bag, and took thence a stone, and slang it, and smote the Philistine in his forehead, that the stone sunk into his forehead; and he fell upon his face to the earth. So David prevailed over the Philistine with a sling and with a stone, and smote the Philistine, and slew him; but there was no sword in the hand of David. Therefore, David ran, and stood upon the Philistine, and took his sword, and drew it out of the sheath thereof, and slew him, and cut off his head therewith. And when the Philistines saw their champion was dead, they fled" (vv. 48-51).

David slew Goliath, the giant Philistine. He was victorious in all of his battles. He became Jonathan's (Saul's son) best friend. He later married Saul's daughter, Michal. But then one day things begin to change, and David found himself under attack by Saul, who made several attempts to take David's life. As a matter of fact, these attacks spanned from the time David took the position as Saul's armor bearer until shortly before Saul's death. Saul resented the relationship his son Jonathan had with David and tried to break it up. Don't forget, David still had an anointing over his life to become king, but he had not taken the throne.

In I Samuel 19:1, Saul put out a contract on David's life. "And Saul spake to Jonathan his son, and to all his servants, *that they should kill David.*" But Jonathan, Saul's son, loved David, and he warned David of his father's plot. So David hid until he received word from Jonathan that it was safe to return. Jonathan spoke with his father and reminded him that David had put his life on the line not only for the king but also for all of Israel. So Saul swore before Jonathan that David would not be slain, and David returned.

"And David went out whithersoever Saul sent him, and behaved himself wisely; and Saul set him over the men of war, and he was accepted in the sight of all the people, and also in the sight of Saul's servants" (I Samuel 18:5).

Another war with the Philistines ensued. David went out and fought with the Philistines and slew them in a great slaughter, and those who remained fled from him.

"And it came to pass as they came, when David was returned from the slaughter of the Philistine, that the women came out of all cities of Israel, singing and dancing, to meet king Saul, with tabrets, with joy, and with instruments of musick. And the women answered one another as they played, and said, Saul hath slain his thousands, and David his ten thousands. And Saul was very wroth, and the saying displeased him; and he said, They have ascribed unto David ten thousands, and to me they have ascribed but thousands: and what can he have more but the kingdom? And Saul eyed David from that day and forward" (I Samuel 18:6-9).

The very next day the evil spirit from God came upon Saul, and David began to play the harp to soothe him as he had done in the past. But the playing of the harp did not soothe him this time, and he took the javelin that was in his hand and threw it at David, but David slipped out of Saul's presence and escaped. The king's javelin smote the wall instead. This was the second time David had escaped from Saul's presence. Now Saul was afraid of David because he recognized that the Lord was with David, and no longer with him. It seemed that no matter how hard he tried to kill David, he was unable.

Saul sent messengers to David's house to watch him and to slay him in the morning. This time Michal, Saul's daughter and David's wife, warned him, and she helped David escape through a window. Saul became furious with his daughter. Hence, David began to live the life of a fugitive—running from a man he has loved as king and father. He found himself *sorting through God's love*, trying to understand why all of this was happening to him when he had done no wrong. Saul's rage and jealousy fueled his motivation to pursue and kill David.

In chapter 20 David met Jonathan again, and he asks Jonathan why his father still wanted to kill him. Jonathan refused to believe that Saul would actually kill David, so he made another agreement with David in an attempt to prove that David had misunderstood Saul. He says,

"…Far be it from thee: for if I knew certainly that evil were determined by my father to come upon thee, then would not I tell it thee?… And Jonathan said unto David, O Lord God of Israel, when I have sounded my father about tomorrow any time, or the third day, and behold, if there be good toward David, and I then send not unto thee, and shew it to thee; The Lord do so and much more to Jonathan: but if it please my father to do thee evil, then I will shew it thee, and send thee away, that thou mayest go in peace: and the Lord be with thee, as he hath been with my father.…So Jonathan made a covenant with the house of David, saying, Let the Lord even require it at the hand of David's enemies. And Jonathan caused David to swear again, because he loved him: *for he loved him as he loved his own soul*" (vv. 9-17).

Jonathan returned and spoke with his father, and Saul enquired as to David's whereabouts. When Jonathan made an excuse for David's absence, Saul was outraged; his anger was kindled once again toward Jonathan.

"...Thou son of the perverse, rebellious woman, do not I know that thou hast chosen the son of Jesse to thine own confusion, and unto the confusion of thy mother's nakedness? For as long as the son of Jesse liveth upon the ground, thou shalt not be established, nor thy kingdom. Wherefore now send and fetch him unto me, *for he shall surely die"* (vv. 30, 31).

Saul had no intentions of letting David take his son's place on the throne as the next king, so he vowed to kill David. This was the last thing Jonathan expected his father to say. "So Jonathan arose from the table in fierce anger, and did eat no food the second day of the month: for he was grieved for David, because his father had done him shame" (v. 34).

Sadness and anguish filled Jonathan's heart at the thought of returning to David only to acknowledge he had learned the truth and surely his father sought to kill David. Once Jonathan's servant had been sent away, he and David were able to meet at David's hiding place. The emotions of the two friends spilled over into sorrow and grief.

"And as soon as the lad was gone, David arose out of a place toward the south, and fell on his face to the ground, and bowed himself three times: and they kissed one another, and wept one with another, until David exceeded [controlled himself]" (v. 41).

Jonathan sent David away as they had sworn, and Jonathan returned to the city.

David continued to flee from Saul, who took three thousand chosen men out of Israel to seek David and his men. At last the time arrived, and David had an opportune moment to take revenge and kill Saul. According to the text in chapter 24, David and his men came upon Saul asleep in a cave. David cut off Saul's skirt without awakening the king, and he restrained his men from rising up against Saul. Then David was overcome with sorrow because of his action; his love for Saul had remained in spite of Saul's pursuit to kill him. He cried out to Saul, asking, "Saul, why you do listen to other men's words who say that I seek to harm you when my actions have proven to be honorable? My loyalty to you has been pure and uncompromised."

It seems like we have been down this path before with Saul. Listening to other people versus listening to God is how he lost the kingdom in the first place.

Saul finally broke and responded to David.

"…Is this thy voice, my son David? And Saul lifted up his voice, and wept. And he said to David, Thou art more righteous than I: for thou hast rewarded me good, whereas I have rewarded thee evil. And thou hast shewed this day how that thou hast dealt well with me: forasmuch as when the LORD had delivered me into thine hand, thou killedst me not" (vv. 16-18).

Saul now saw David as he had when he first met him; he saw him as his beloved son. But this emotional display of love was brief. Soon after this eloquent little speech, Saul began anew his pursuit to kill David.

David, on the other hand, returned to war to fight another battle. In the battle, David's city, Ziklag, was invaded and burned. All of the women and the wives and children of David and his men were taken captive by the Amalekites.

David became greatly distressed because the people spoke of stoning him. Every man was grieved at the loss of his family, "…*but David encouraged himself in the* LORD *his God*" (I Samuel 30:6). He sought counsel from God and returned to battle again, recovering all that the Amalekites had carried away. He recovered his two wives as well as the sons, daughters and wives of the men. David recovered everything that had been taken, as well as all the flocks and herds and cattle that belonged to the Amalekites as spoil (I Samuel 30:17-20).

David's victory celebration was cut short, and his heart was grieved as he learned of the deaths of Saul and Jonathan. David paid special tribute to Saul, his king, and his friend, Jonathan.

"Saul and Jonathan were lovely and pleasant in their lives, and in their death were they not divided: they were swifter than eagles, they were stronger than lions.... I am distressed for thee, my brother Jonathan: very pleasant hast thou been unto me: thy love to me was wonderful, passing the love of women" (2 Samuel 1:23-25).

Not until David experienced the deaths of his beloved friend and confidant, Jonathan, and King Saul, the man he had loved as his own father, did he walk into the anointing God had for him. God's timing is not our timing. God knows exactly what Babylon experience He will take us through to purge us and make us greater fruit-bearing vessels for His glory.

II Samuel 2:4, "And the men of Judah came, and there they anointed David king over the house of Judah...." *Talk about the discipline of delay!*

Seemingly David deserved a little peace, but God said, "Not so." David's life was not a life of peace; it was a life of war. After the death of Saul and Jonathan, a long war ensued between the house of Saul and the house of David. "Now there was a long war between the house of Saul and the house of David; but David grew stronger and stronger, and the house of Saul grew weaker and weaker" (II Samuel 3:1). Finally, after many long battles, David was anointed as king of Israel.

"So all the elders [leaders] of Israel came to the king to Hebron; and king David made a league with them in Hebron before the LORD: and they anointed David king over Israel. David was thirty years old when he began to reign, and he reigned forty years. In Hebron he reigned over Judah seven years and six months: and in Jerusalem he reigned thirty and three years over all Israel and Judah" (II Samuel 5:3-5).

David then began his family, and his wives and concubines gave birth to both sons and daughters. So he has a brief moment of joy and celebration of fatherhood, but David goes to war with the Philistines again. "…when the Philistines heard that they had anointed David king over Israel, all the Philistines came up to seek David; and David heard of it, and went down to the [strong]hold" (II Samuel 5:17).

"And David enquired of the LORD, saying, Shall I go up to the Philistines? wilt thou deliver them into mind hand? and the LORD said unto David, Go up: for I will doubtless deliver the Philistines into thine hand" (II Samuel 5:19).

Even after this battle, David continued to be plagued with the Philistines, and he fought battle after battle. Finally, God gave David rest from his enemies:

"And it came to pass, when the king sat in his house, and the LORD had given him rest round about from all his enemies; That the king said unto Nathan the prophet, See now, I dwell in an house of cedar, but the ark of God dwelleth within curtains" (II Samuel 7:1, 2).

After God gave David rest from his enemies, he began to ponder ways he could bless God. David desired to build a sanctuary for the ark of God to reside, and he believed this was his opportunity to bless God. So he assembled all of the princes of Israel, the princes of the tribes, captains, stewards, his sons and all his officers and the mighty and valiant men to come before him to make an announcement.

"Then David the king, stood upon his feet, and said, Hear me, my brethren, and my people: As for me, I had in mine heart to build an house of rest for the ark of the covenant of the LORD, and for the footstool of our God, and had made ready for the building: But God said unto me, Thou shalt not build an house for my name, because thou hast been a man of war, and hast shed blood. Howbeit, the LORD God of Israel chose me before all the house of my father to be king over Israel for ever: for he hath chosen Judah to be the ruler; and of the house of Judah, the house of my father; and among the sons of my father he liked me to make me king over all Israel: And of all my sons (for the LORD hath given me many sons,) he hath chosen Solomon, my son, to sit upon the throne of the kingdom of the LORD over Israel. And he said unto me, Solomon thy son, he shall build my house and my courts: for I have chosen him to be my son, and I will be his father" (I Chronicles 28:2-6).

David prepared Solomon for the job.

"Then he called for Solomon his son, and charged him to build an house for the LORD God of Israel. And David said to Solomon, My son, as for me, it was in my mind to build an house unto the name of the LORD my God. But the word of the LORD came to me, saying, Thou hast shed blood abundantly, and hast made great wars: thou shalt not build an house unto my name, because thou hast shed much blood upon the earth in my sight. Behold, a son shall be born to thee, who shall be a man of rest; and I will give him rest from all his enemies round about: for his name shall be Solomon, and I will give peace and quietness unto Israel in his days. He shall build an house for my name..." (I Chronicles 22:6-10).

Even though God loved David, He knew His divine purpose for David. God never intended for David to be a man of peace. David's hands had been equipped with an anointing of that of a warrior—not a peacemaker.

David not only experienced war outside of his home on battlefields and within the house of Saul, but he also experienced war in his own house. David's son Amnon sinned against his half-sister Tamar by raping her.

"And it came to pass after this, that Absalom the son of David had a fair sister, whose name was Tamar; and Amnon, the son of David, loved her. And Amnon was so vexed [distressed] that he fell sick for his sister Tamar; for she was a virgin; and Amnon thought it hard for him to do anything to her" (II Samuel 13:1, 2).

In verse 4, Amnon confided his love for his sister to a friend named Jonadab. "And he said unto him, Why art thou, being the king's son, lean from day to day? wilt thou not tell me? And Amnon said unto him, I love Tamar, my brother Absalom's sister."

Jonadab developed a scheme and convinced Amnon to pretend to be sick to lure Tamar to his bedside.

"And Jonadab said unto him, Lay thee down on thy bed, and make thyself sick: and when thy father cometh to see thee, say unto him, I pray thee, let my sister Tamar come, and give me meat, and dress [prepare] the food in my sight, that I may see it, and eat at her hand" (II Samuel 13:5).

So Tamar went to Amnon's house and prepared cakes before him. She took the food into his chamber as he had requested of her

"And when she had brought them unto him to eat, he took hold of her, and said unto her, Come lie with me, my sister. And she answered him, Nay, my brother, do not force me; for no such thing ought to be done in Israel: do not thou this folly…. Howbeit, he would not hearken unto her voice: but, being stronger than she, forced her, and lay with her. Then Amnon hated her exceedingly; so that the hatred wherewith he hated her was greater than the love wherewith he had loved her. And Amnon said unto her, Arise, be gone" (II Samuel 13:11-15).

When Absalom heard of his brother Amnon's violation of his sister, he became very angry and refused to speak to his brother because he had forced his sister. Absalom's anger brewed for two years, and he yearned for an opportunity to avenge his sister. One day when all of the king's sons were gathered together, Absalom sought the opportunity to kill Amnon.

"Now Absalom had commanded his servants, saying, Mark ye now, when Amnon's heart is merry with wine, and when I say unto you, Smite Amnon; then kill him, fear not: have not I commanded you? be courageous, and be valiant. And the servants of Absalom did unto Amnon as Absalom had commanded…" (II Samuel 13:28, 29).

Out of all the wars David experienced, the war raging among his children was the greatest. David experienced war, death and division in his own household among his children.

At this point David experienced the jealousy of Absalom at the level he did with King Saul. Absalom had watched his father David rule and judge Israel for forty years, and he yearned to have the same appeal and love of the people that was shown his father. "Absalom said moreover, Oh that *I* were made judge in the land, *that every man who hath any suit or cause might come unto me,* and I would do him justice!" (2 Samuel 15:4).

Soon Absalom stole the hearts of the men of Israel, and he encouraged the men of Israel to ascribe honor to his name and not to his father. A conspiracy was formed, and the men of Israel along with Absalom rose up against David.

"And there came a messenger to David, saying, The hearts of the men of Israel are after Absalom" (v. 13). Once again David took flight on the run for his life. However, this time the enemy was not Saul. The enemy is not from the camp without; it is from the camp within—from his own beloved son, Absalom.

"And David said unto all his servants who were with him at Jerusalem, Arise, and let us flee; for we shall not else escape from Absalom: make speed to depart, lest he overtake us suddenly, and bring evil upon us, and smite the city with the edge of the sword" (v. 14).

In reading the account of David's battles in the books of I and II Samuel and I and II Chronicles, we are given a glimpse of what David encountered in his lifetime. Now let's return to the book of Psalms to see how David responded to the will of God in his life, his relationships and his sufferings. Let's see if David still desires to bless the Lord at all times.

David began to write psalms, hymns and spiritual songs to God and about God out of the depths of his soul as he lives his life of turmoil on the run. He penned some of the most vivid accounts of what a man experiences in his heart when he is going though mountaintop and death-valley experiences all at the hand of an all-loving and merciful God.

Of the 150 Psalms, 73 Psalms are attributed to David. David is believed to have written the first 42 Psalms. The third Psalm was written by David when he fled from Absalom. David said: "Lord, how are they increased that trouble me! many are they that rise up against me. Many there be which say of my soul, There is no help for him in God. Selah" (vv. 1, 2).

Then David cried out in the fourth Psalm:

"Hear me when I call, O God of my righteousness: thou hast enlarged me when I was in distress; have mercy upon me, and hear my prayer....I will both lay me down in peace, and sleep: for thou, LORD, only makest me dwell in safety" (vv. 1, 8).

David's plea to God is that God would protect him from Absalom. Can you imagine praying for protection from your own son? Imagine how David felt... He had grown up having the utmost respect for his father and never having had such an evil thought against his own father, yet his own son was rising up against him, seeking to murder him out of jealousy. Can you feel his pain? He was a man who had fought for God all his life, and it appears this is the way God has chosen to respond to him.

In spite of all of his pain, he declared, "But as for me, I will come into thy house in the multitude of thy mercy: and in thy fear will I worship toward thy holy temple" (Psalm 5:7). David blessed God in the midst of his pain. Even when David was confused and perplexed over his circumstances, he still acknowledged God saying, "O LORD my God, in thee do I put my trust..." (Psalm 7:1). He was saying, "I don't understand what You are doing, but I trust You. I trust Your love for me."

Even when God subjected David to the discipline of delay in the thirteenth Psalm, David said, "I will sing unto the Lord, because he hath dealt bountifully with me" (v. 6). But he began the Psalm by saying,

"How long wilt thou forget me, O LORD? Forever? how long wilt thou hide thy face from me? How long shall I take counsel in my soul, having sorrow in my heart daily? how long shall mine enemy be exalted over me?"

Psalm 8 contains that famous Scripture in which David gave glory to God saying, *"O LORD, our Lord, how excellent is thy name in all the earth! who hast set thy glory above the heavens!"* (v. 1). And David began to praise God saying, *"I will praise thee, O LORD, with my whole heart; I will shew forth all thy marvelous works. I will be glad and rejoice in thee: I will sing praise to thy name, O thou most High"* (Psalm 9:1, 2). *"I will bless the LORD, who hath given me counsel...* (Psalm 16:7).

David had learned the path of life and joy was in God's presence, *"Thou wilt shew me the path of life: in thy presence is fulness of joy; at thy right hand there are pleasures for evermore"* Psalm 16:11). He had experienced God's hand of deliverance: *"He delivered me from my strong enemy, and from them which hated me: for they were too strong for me"* (Psalm 18:17). David learned the works and Word of God through his battles. He learned he was not wise enough to interpret the judgment and the ways of God, and he dared not speak that which he did not understand about the living God. Instead, he prayed, *"Let the words of my mouth, and the meditation of my heart, be acceptable in thy sight, O LORD, my strength, and my redeemer"* (Psalm 19:14).

David had become weary to the point that his soul and his bones were vexed. His enemies had pursued him all of his life—even though he had done them no wrong. He could run no more. He repeatedly cried out to God to deliver him from those who oppressed him. Yet a common thread weaves throughout the chapters leading up to the thirty-fourth Psalm. Somehow David never lost his complete trust in God. He never stopped praising God for His mighty acts. He continued to seek God for a refuge and a fortress. He never doubted God's intentions or God's love for him.

I believe the greatest account of David's extolling God is found in the twenty-third and the thirty-fourth Psalms.

In the twenty-third Psalm, David wrote:

"The LORD is my shepherd; I shall not want.

He maketh me to lie down in green pastures; he leadeth me beside the still waters.

He restoreth my soul: he leadeth me in the paths of righteousness for his name's sake.

Yea, though I walk through the valley of the shadow of death, I will fear no evil: for thou art with me; thy rod and thy staff they comfort me.

Thou preparest a table before me in the presence of mine enemies: thou anointest my head with oil; my cup runneth over.

Surely goodness and mercy shall follow me all the days of my life: and I will dwell in the house of the LORD forever."

In spite of all he had lived through and all he had seen in his life, David emerged from his death-valley experiences with mountaintop professions of God's goodness. He had learned there is none like God. God reigned!

God is fair and just in all His ways. God is righteous. David compared God to a great Shepherd. He knew God as One who cared for and provided guidance to His people. He knew God as his Teacher and his Protector. There was no way for David to know this without having had an intimate relationship with God through the experiences God allowed (permissive will) and sent (divine will) him through.

In the face of his enemies, David had experienced God's protection and deliverance. David knew God's anointing was over his life. He knew God's presence abided in him. He knew God had consecrated him. He had been dedicated by God through the prophet Samuel to a specific given goal and service through the act of pouring the spiritual oil of sacrament, separating him at an early age for God's service.

And finally in portions of the thirty-fourth Psalm, David made an oath and a promise:

"I will bless the LORD at all times: his praise shall continually be in my mouth.

My soul shall make her boast the LORD: the humble shall hear thereof, and be glad.

O magnify the LORD with me, and let us exalt his name together.

I sought the LORD, and he heard me, and delivered me from all my fears.

O taste and see that the LORD is good: blessed is the man that trusteth in him.

The eyes of the LORD are upon the righteous, and his ears are open unto their cry.

The righteous cry, and the LORD heareth, and delivereth them out of all their troubles.

The LORD is nigh [near] unto them that are of a broken heart; and saveth such as be of a contrite spirit.

Many are the afflictions of the righteous: but the LORD delivereth him out of them all.

The LORD redeemeth the soul of his servants; and none of them that trust in him shall be desolate."

Do you think David knew what he was writing about? Do you think he wrote about what he had *heard* or what he *knew* about God? Obviously he wrote about what he knew because he had lived through fear and he had walked through the valley and the shadow of death and learned the only way of escape was through his faith and trust in almighty Jehovah.

David knew what it felt like to cry all night long. He had slept out in the wilderness with a rock for a pillow and the ground for a bed because he was no longer welcomed in his own home. He wrote what he knew because he had lived with a broken heart for much of his life. He had experienced rejection and hatred from those he loved most, but most of all, he wrote what he knew because he had experienced the deliverance of a loving and caring God.

David declared that the afflictions of the righteous are great; as a matter of fact, they are so great that they were more than the number of hairs on his head. He could no longer count them, but he knew he served and loved a God who was not only his Shepherd, but his Redeemer, his Rock and his Refuge. He served and loved a God who would never—no, not ever—leave him alone.

Many are the Afflictions

David declared, *"Surely goodness and mercy shall follow me all the days of my life: and I will dwell in the house of the* LORD *forever."*

We have learned what *"I will bless you at all times—a promise from man to God"* means. What does *"I will bless you at all times—a promise from God to man"* connote?

"Now the LORD HAD said unto Abram, Get thee out of thy country, and from thy kindred, and from thy father's house, unto a land that I will shew thee: And I will make of thee a great nation, and I will bless thee, and make thy name great; and thou shalt be a blessing: And I will bless them that bless thee, and curse him that curseth thee: an in thee shall all families of the earth be blessed" (Genesis 12:1-3).

In the preceding verses, God made a covenant agreement and a promise to bless Abram. What you may not realize are the conditions under which the blessings of God were given and to whom the blessings apply.

When God made the promise, He made the promise not only to bless Abraham but to bless Abram's seed. That seed represented the nation of Israel, the church of Jesus Christ and to the Gentile nations.

First, let's look at the promise to bless Israel:

"In the same day the LORD made a covenant with Abram, saying, Unto thy seed have I given this land, from the river of Egypt unto the great river, the river Euphrates. The Kenites, and the Kenizzites, and the Kadmonites, And the Hittites, and the Perizzites, and the Rephaims, And the Amorites, and the Canaanites, and the Girgashites, and the Jebusites" (Genesis 15:18-21).

And says to Abram,

"And I will establish my covenant between me and thee and thy seed after thee in their generations for an everlasting covenant, to be a God unto thee, and to thy seed after thee. And I will give unto thee, and to thy seed after thee, the land wherein thou art a stranger, all the land of Canaan, for an everlasting possession; and I will be their God" (Genesis 17:7, 8).

God made a promise of blessings through Abram's seed of ownership a vast land and a specific territory.

Secondly, God made a promise to bless the church. Paul provided an account of this promise in Galatians 3:

"Now to Abraham and his seed were the promises made. He saith not, And to seeds, as of many; but as of one, And to thy seed, which is Christ.... There is neither Jew nor Greek, there is neither bond nor free, there is neither male nor female; for ye are one in Christ Jesus. And if ye be Christ's, then are ye Abraham's seed, and heirs according to the promise" (vv. 16, 28, 29).

This promise is not made to the church based on denomination. It is made to one *Church*, Jesus Christ. Christ is the Church—not the building nor the denomination. Those who are saved in Christ Jesus make up the church and inherit the promise and the blessing. Through the seed of one man, Abram, was the promise made, and through the birth of one man, Jesus Christ, was the promise fulfilled.

Thirdly, God made a promise to bless the Gentile nations when He said, "And I will bless them that bless thee, and curse him that curseth thee: and in thee shall all families of the earth be blessed" (Genesis 12:3). How can God fulfill such a promise? He fulfills His promise in the birth, death and resurrection of His Son, Jesus Christ. The lineage began in Abram, whom God later renamed *Abraham*.

Abraham and his wife, Sarah, gave birth to a son name Isaac, and God revisited His promise in Genesis 17:19, "And God said, Sarah thy wife shall bear thee a son indeed; and thou shalt call his name Isaac: and I will establish my covenant with him for an everlasting covenant, and with his seed after him." So who carried the seed after Isaac?

Follow me to Genesis 24:60. Isaac grew up and married a girl named Rebekah, who received a prophetic blessing over her life when she was sent away to become Isaac's wife. The Scripture reads, "And they blessed Rebekah, and said unto her, Thou art our sister, be thou the mother of thousands of millions, and let thy seed possess the gate of those which hate them." Isaac and Rebekah gave birth to a son name Jacob. Isaac blessed Jacob with the blessing of God. God visited Jacob in a dream and declared:

"And thy seed shall be as the dust of the earth, and thou shalt spread abroad to the west, and to the east, and to the north, and to the south: and in thee and in thy seed shall all the families of the earth be blessed" (Genesis 28:14).

So who was in the lineage of Jacob?

The promise is fulfilled through Abraham's seed through the birth of Jesus Christ. Christ was begat through Abraham and Jacob's seed through several generations who eventually give birth to Obed, the father of Jesse, who was the father of David, and Mary was in the lineage of David. Mary is the mother of Jesus Christ.

"Now the birth of Jesus Christ was on this wise: When as his mother Mary was espoused to Joseph, before they came together, she was found with child of the Holy Ghost. And she shall bring forth a son, and thou shalt call his name Jesus: for he shall save his people from their sins" (Matthew 1:18, 21).

This, of course, was a progressive event over a course or time: "So all the generations from Abraham to David are fourteen generations;

and from David until the carrying away into Babylon are fourteen generations; and from the carrying away into Babylon unto Christ are fourteen generations" (Matthew 1:17). Here we see the fulfillment of the promise of God to bless the seed of Jacob through the birth of Jesus Christ as He promised. Christ provided the Gentile nation with access to all the inherited promises and blessings God gave Abram.

God made an addendum to the contract He made with Israel, saying to the Gentile nation, "If you bless Israel, I will bless you." Who are the Gentiles? A *Gentile* is "anyone who is not of the Jewish faith or is of a non-Jewish nation." God says, "Nothing shall be withheld from you. God will bless you with the same blessings which He blessed Israel."

As Gentiles in the church age, we are called upon to trust God as Abram did whereby we are able to receive the same blessings in the covenant between God and Abram. Why? *Because God desires to bless us at all times.*

According to Deuteronomy 28:1-14, God gives us a clear indication of how we can be blessed:

"And it shall come to pass, if thou shalt hearken diligently unto the voice of the LORD thy God, to observe and do all his commandments which I command thee this day, that the LORD thy God will set thee on high above all nations of the earth:

And all these blessings shall come on thee, and overtake thee, if thou shalt hearken unto the voice of the LORD thy God.

Blessed shalt thou be in the city, and blessed shalt thou be in the field.

Blessed shall be the fruit of thy body, and the fruit of thy ground, and the fruit of thy cattle, the increase of thy kine, and the flocks of thy sheep.

Blessed shall be thy basket and thy store.

Blessed shalt thou be when thou comest in, and blessed shalt thou be when thou goest out.

The LORD shall cause thine enemies who rise up against thee to be smitten before thy face: they shall come out against thee one way, and flee before thee seven ways.

The LORD shall command the blessings upon thee in thy storehouses, and in all that thou settest thine hand unto; and he shall bless thee in the land which the LORD thy God giveth thee.

The LORD shall establish thee an holy people unto himself, as he hath sworn unto thee, if thou shalt keep the commandments of the LORD thy God, and walk in his ways.

And all the people of the earth shall see that thou art called by the name of the LORD, and they shall be afraid of thee.

And the LORD shall make thee plenteous in goods, in the fruit of thy body, and in the fruit of thy cattle, and in the fruit of thy ground, in the land which the LORD sware unto thy fathers to give thee.

The LORD shall open unto thee his good treasure, the heaven to give the rain unto thy land in his season, and to bless all the work of thine hand: and thou shalt lend unto many nations, and thou shalt not borrow.

And the LORD shall make thee the head, and not the tail; and thou shalt be above only, and thou shalt not be beneath; if that thou hearken unto the commandments of the LORD thy God, which I command thee this day, to observe and to do them."

The above referenced Scripture lets you know these are the things that bring the blessings of God into your life. I will make a strong admonishment at this point and say, "Whatever you do, don't walk away from this chapter limiting the blessings of God by putting God in a box!" God not only desires to bless you with temporal blessing of houses, land and the riches of this world, but He desires to bless you with spiritual blessings that are everlasting, that cannot be purchased with gold. *God is bigger than the tangible!*

God's spiritual blessings will always prevail over the blessings that are perishable. Spiritual blessings are the result of the sacrificial atonement and death on the cross of His Son, Jesus Christ. As a spiritual blessing, God declares us righteous through His Son. God blesses us with faith, hope, love, and joy that no man can give, and no man can take away because it's not tangible; it's intangible. We cannot physically touch hope or love because they are spiritual forces that abide in us through the presence of the Holy Spirit. The power of the Holy Spirit energizes us when we feel we cannot go on. That power is none other than the Holy Spirit, who enlarges our vision of God and the power of God to work in our circumstances when our conditions say there is no hope and no reason to keep pressing toward the mark. When all around us is destruction, devastation and deterioration, God blesses us with His peace that passes all understanding.

John prayed in the third epistle of John: "Beloved, I wish above all things that thou mayest prosper and be in health, even as thy soul prospereth" (v. 2). John knew God was interested not only in our physical prosperity and our bodily condition, God was interested more in the condition of our soul. A prosperous soul is a spiritual blessing that can come only from God. You cannot buy it with silver or gold, so he prayed this verse for his friend Gaius. If you want to pray for your friends, do as John did and pray for the prosperity of their soul—not just for their health and wealth to accumulate fortune and fame.

Now you have your own testimony and you can declare to the world that *the task is not easy; God never promised that it would be. It just looks easy because God enables me to do the task with ease. He just keeps on blessing me.*

Just ask David; he'll tell you.

CHAPTER SEVEN

I'VE GOT YOUR BACK

"Now it came to pass in the days when the judges ruled, that there was a famine in the land. And a certain man of Bethlehemjudah went to sojourn in the country of Moab, he, and his wife, and his two sons. And the name of the man was Elimelech, and the name of his wife, Naomi, and the name of his two sons, Mahlon and Chilion, Ephrathites of Bethlehemjudah. And they came into the country of Moab, and continued there. And Elimelech, Naomi's husband died; and she was left, and her two sons. And they took themselves wives of the women of Moab; the name of one was Orpah, and the name of the other Ruth: and they dwelled there about ten years. And Mahlon and Chilion died also both of them; and the woman was left of her two sons and her husband" (Ruth 1:1-5).

In this Scripture, a Jewess named Naomi traveled with her husband and sons to the foreign land of Moab, only to become a widow in that foreign land. A long history of hostility and fighting existed between Israel and Moab. Nonetheless, Naomi and her husband made a good home for their sons in Moab, so she abides in Moab after the death of her husband with her sons. While living in the land of Moab, her sons married women of Moab. Ten years later, both sons died, leaving the widow-women childless. Naomi was left with two Moabite daughters-in-law.

Naomi spoke to her daughters-in-law to let them know how much she appreciated all they had done. The daughters-in-law stayed with her after the death of her sons (their husbands), but she recognized that they were beautiful young women with much potential to marry again and bear children. So she bade them to return to their own mother's house as she made preparation to return to Bethlehem in Judah.

After much resistance, Orpah heeded the instruction of Naomi and returned to her people of Moab. But Ruth refused to leave Naomi. The Scripture recorded Ruth's reply:

"And Ruth said, Intreat me not to leave thee, or to return from following after thee; for whither thou goest, I will go; and where thou lodgest, I will lodge: thy people shall be my people, and thy God, my God: Where thou diest, will I die, and there will I be buried: the LORD do so to me, and more also, if ought but death part thee and me" (Ruth 1:16, 17).

Finally, Naomi accepted the fact that she could not persuade Ruth to go back to her people of Moab. So the two of them journey back to Bethlehem. Once they arrived in Bethlehem, Naomi changed her name to *Mara*, meaning "the Almighty hath dealt very bitterly with me." Ruth immediately realized they must have an income and food to eat. Ruth set out to work by gleaning in the fields of Boaz, a kinsman of her former father-in-law, Elimelech. "And Ruth, the Moabitess, said unto Naomi, Let me now go to the field, and glean ears of grain after him in whose sight I shall find grace. And she said unto her, Go, my daughter" (Ruth 2:2).

But God had plans for this widowed Moabitess and her mother-in-law. Even though they felt like they were all alone, and they would live as beggars and paupers God had already begun to turn their situation around. Theirs was an unusual way for God to demonstrate *He had their back*, nonetheless He did.

Naomi was an old woman; she knew her homeland would be a better place to live. Nonetheless, she also knew that returning with a Moabite daughter-in-law would ostracize her from her former friends and family. After all, the Moabites were enemies of Israel. But Naomi pressed on and returned to Bethlehem with Ruth at her side.

Once arriving in Bethlehem, Ruth took charge of the situation, recognizing they had no way to feed and take care of themselves. So Ruth began to glean in the field after the reapers, which was common practice for women when they had no means to take care of themselves. Boaz took notice of her:

"Then said Boaz unto his servant who was set over the reapers, Whose damsel is this? And the servant who was set over the reapers answered and said, It is the Moabitish damsel that came back with Naomi out of the country of Moab: And she said, I pray you, let me glean and gather after the reapers among the sheaves: so she came, and hath continued even from morning until now, except that she tarried a little in the house" (Ruth 2:5-7).

Boaz's heart became passionate toward Ruth, and he told her to stay close to his maidens and to reap in the same fields as his maidens. He charged the young men not to touch her and when she became thirsty she was to drink from the vessels that the young men had drawn. This courtesy and kindness being extended to a Moabite was highly unusual for a man of Israel. Boaz knew Ruth was not accepted by the people of Bethlehem and that she had not been made to feel welcome. But he saw a type of love in Ruth that he had never seen before. He had seen her love demonstrated for her mother-in-law in the face of opposition, ridicule, scorn and rejection. Hers was a pure, unselfish love.

Overcome with thanksgiving, Ruth fell on her face, bowed herself to the ground, and asked Boaz, "...Why have I found grace in thine eyes, that thou shouldest take knowledge of me, seeing I am a foreigner?" (v. 10).

Boaz responded saying, "...It hath fully been shewed me, all that thou hast done for thy mother in law since the death of thine husband: and how thou hast left thy father and thy mother, and the land of thy nativity, and art come unto a people whom thou knewest not heretofore."

Then God stepped in to let Ruth know, "I've got your back!" Boaz spoke blessings over Ruth's life saying, "The Lord recompense thy work, and a full reward be given thee by the LORD God of Israel, under whose wings thou art come to trust." You see even though Ruth was not an Israelite, she had learned about God through the life of Naomi. She had learned who God was through her mother-in-law. Ruth had begun to worship Jehovah God as her God. She had trusted the God of Israel to take care of her and to provide for her and Naomi.

Boaz went even further and invited Ruth to eat with the reapers. While she was eating, Boaz noticed the grain she has gleaned was dried out and burnt by the sun. After all, she was getting the left-over grain that the reapers left behind because it was no good.

Boaz's heart was melting quickly, and he instructed his reapers to let her glean among the sheaves and not to reproach her. As a matter of fact, he told them, "I want you to purposefully let some of the good grain you have picked fall to the ground. When Ruth comes behind you, she will see it and pick it up. When she does, do her no harm."

As Ruth returned home at the end of a long day, she shared her story with Naomi, who was happy for he daughter-in-law. However, she was also concerned for her safety and warned Ruth to continue to go out with the maidens of Boaz, but only in the fields of Boaz. She was not to meet with these maidens in any other fields.

Naomi knew these maidens had watched Ruth and had seen the favoritism shown her by Boaz. More than likely they were very jealous of her. So she warned her daughter-in-law how to govern herself. God used Naomi. In today's vernacular, Naomi told Ruth, *"I've got your back."*

God continues to use people to warn His children of impending danger and opposition. But many people ignore the warning because they cannot receive instruction from others. They simply do not like others telling them what they should or should not do. As a result, they walk right into situations that cause them great anguish and heartache. Ruth was willing to listen to wise counsel. She had watched Naomi and had seen the consistency in her walk before Jehovah God. She yearned to have the same relationship with the God of Israel that Naomi had.

Being a woman of purpose and destiny, Naomi saw an opportunity for Ruth. Naomi was well-acquainted with the customs of Israel. She knew the kinsmen of a widow woman are to buy the field of that widow and to take the widow as his wife in order to raise up the name of the dead husband so there would continue to be an inheritance in the lineage. The dead man's name would not be cut off from among his family. Therefore, Naomi positioned Ruth to attract Boaz. "Then Naomi her mother in law said unto her, My daughter, shall I not seek rest for thee, that it may be well with thee?" (Ruth 3:1).

Naomi instructed Ruth to wash and anoint herself and to put on attractive raiment. She was to go down to the threshing floor where Boaz would be, but Naomi told her to be very discreet and not to make herself known. Once Boaz had eaten and drank and had retired to rest for the night, she was to uncover his feet and lie at his feet. Ruth was obedient and followed Naomi's exact instructions.

"And it came to pass at midnight, that the man was afraid, and turned himself: and, behold, a woman lay at his feet. And he said, Who art thou? And she answered, I am Ruth thine handmaid: spread therefore thy skirt over thine handmaid; for thou art a near kinsman" (Ruth 3:8, 9).

Boaz recognized Ruth, blessed her and acknowledged the invitation she had extended to him. He knew that this gesture was an appeal from Ruth to be his wife.

He knew the custom of the land was for the male who was the nearest of kin to the widow's dead husband to take the widow in marriage. In this case, Boaz advised Ruth that there was another eligible kinsman, and before he can step into the role of her husband, he would need to meet with the other kinsman.

So the next morning Boaz waited at the gate in anticipation of seeing this other kinsman. Sure enough, the other kinsman of whom he had spoken to Ruth passed by. Boaz greeted the other kinsman and bade him sit down. He also took ten other men of the elders of the city and had then sit with them as witnesses.

Boaz explained the situation with Naomi and Ruth to the other kinsman, reminding the kinsman of his obligation to purchase the land Naomi owned to ensure it stayed within the family.

"And he said unto the kinsman, Naomi, that is come again out of the country of Moab, selleth a parcel of land, which was our brother Elimelech's; And I thought to advertise [tell] thee, saying, Buy it before the inhabitants, and before the elders of my people. If thou wilt redeem it, redeem it: but if thou wilt not redeem it, then tell me, that I may know: for there is none to redeem it beside thee; and I am after thee. And he said, I will redeem it" (Ruth 4:3, 4).

Boaz, anticipating this response added more to the purchase deal.

"Then said Boaz, What day thou buyest the field of the hand of Naomi, thou must buy it also of Ruth, the Moabitess, the wife of the dead, to raise up the name of the dead upon his inheritance.

And the kinsman said, I cannot redeem it for myself, lest I mar mine own inheritance: redeem thou my right to thyself; for I cannot redeem it" (Ruth 4:5, 6).

This, of course, is what Boaz expected the kinsman to say, and it pleased him that he would be the kinsman who would marry Ruth. Boaz acknowledged he had not only purchased all that was Elimelech's and that which his sons owned at the hand of Naomi, but he had also purchased the Moabitess Ruth to be his wife and to raise up the name of the dead for an inheritance so that the name of the dead would not be cut off from the dead man's family.

"So Boaz took Ruth, and she was his wife; and when he went in unto her, the LORD gave her conception, and she bare a son. And the women said unto Naomi, Blessed be the LORD, which hath not left thee this day without a kinsman, that his name may be famous in Israel. And he shall be unto thee a restorer of thy life, and a nourisher of thine old age: for thy daughter in law, which loveth thee, which is better to thee than seven sons, hath born him" (Ruth 4:13-15).

God used a simple Moabite girl in a foreign land to illustrate His love. When it seemed like life had turned its back on an old woman and a young woman full of life and potential, God stepped in and said, "*I've got your back*. I sent you back to the land of promise, so I could bless you. I sent you back to the land in which My covenant agreed abides."

Sometimes God does the same thing with us. He sends us back to a situation or a condition that may appear to be hopeless and lifeless in order to make us complete in Him. He sends us back because there are lessons we need to learn, habits we need to break and tasks we must perform.

He sends us back because He knows healing and restoration will never be ours if we do not return to face our past. He knows facing our past will liberate us to experience our future He has planned for us.

If we would be like Ruth and listen to Godly instruction and receive the wise counsel God sends through others, we would be more victorious in our daily Christian walk.

Because of Ruth's obedience, God blessed her to give birth to Obed, the grandfather of David, the warrior and writer of many of the Psalms addressed in chapter six, and the lineage in which Jesus Christ was born. Boaz represents Christ in that he was Ruth's kinsman-redeemer. Ruth represents the believer. Christ is our kinsman-redeemer. Christ paid the price to redeem us with His blood. God fulfilled His purpose in Ruth and rewarded her for her obedience, devotion and loyalty.

God still seeks to reward those who are obedient, devoted and loyal to Him and His purpose. He seeks to find those who will trust Him— even when they do not understand Him or agree with His decisions. He seeks to find those that rest assured knowing *God's got their back*.

This story is really an illustration of God's love demonstrated and manifested in the lives of two ladies. God taught these two ladies, *"I've got your back" through the manifestation of His divine love for them.* Ruth's capacity to love Naomi was like that of the love demonstrated between David and Jonathan. The unselfish love between Ruth and Naomi demonstrated the love between Naomi and Jehovah God and God and His people, Israel, and even Boaz and Ruth. *It is a love of redemption.* It is that redemptive love that God has for you and to love those who have been despised and rejected. *It is a spiritual love.*

The apostle Paul put it this way, "And hope maketh not ashamed; because the love of God is shed abroad in our hearts by the Holy Spirit which is given unto us" (Romans 5:5). This love is a divine love fashioned into the transformed heart by the Holy Spirit. This love flows out in the power of the Holy Spirit. That's why it is a spiritual love. It is unforced and spontaneous toward its objects. That's why Boaz was able to love Ruth the first time he saw her. He did not see her culture when he looked at her; he saw the woman that she was. He saw the love of God manifested in her countenance.

What is your capacity to love? Do you allow the love of God to penetrate your heart that others may experience God's divine love through you as Naomi did? God says that each one of us has the capacity not only to experience His divine love by having an intimate relationship with Him, but we have the same capacity to extend that love to others through the power of His Holy Spirit. God's love of redemption is available to all who will receive it.

Lord, bless us to receive Your divine love. Then bless us to share Your divine love with others.

In Jesus name,

Amen.

CHAPTER EIGHT

HIS YOKE IS EASY

Yoke *[noun]* 1) A contoured crossbar with two U-shaped pieces that encircle the necks of a pair of oxen, mules, or other draft animals working in a team, b.) A pair of draft animals working as a team, 2) A frame or crossbar designed to be carried across a person's shoulders with equal loads suspended from each end, 3) Something that connects or joins together. To force into heavy labor, bondage, or subjugation. (The American Heritage Dictionary)

Yoke *[verb]* 1) To fit or join with a yoke, 2) To connect, join, or bind together. (The American Heritage Dictionary)

Yoke *[synonyms]* 1) burden, 2) bondage, 3) oppression, and 4) grievous

"*I am* the LORD your God, which brought you forth *out of the land of Egypt,* that ye should not be their bondmen [slaves]; and I have *broken the bands of your yoke,* and made you go *upright*" (Leviticus 26:13).

If I were to interpret the above verse, I would say, "Yahweh, I AM has brought you into the open out from that which was dark, desolate and destructive, that you would no longer be imprisoned to them that seek to keep you hostage to their personal gain; I have busted up those things that have constrained you. I have destroyed the cords that bind you to sin and death, and I have made you to stand up straight."

God had spoken to Moses and given him instructions to give to the children of Israel. These were conditions of blessings and warnings of chastisement. God knew being under the yoke of anyone or anything other than God would be grievous and burdensome. Therefore, He wanted His people to make wise choices and well-planned decisions that would not cause self-imposed burdens and hardship.

God delivered His people out from under the wicked rule of Pharaoh in Egypt. They had been enslaved to Pharaoh 430 years. "Now sojourning of the children of Israel, who dwelt in Egypt, was four hundred and thirty years" (Exodus 12:40).

And the Lord said to Moses in Exodus 20:2, "I am the LORD thy God, which have brought thee out of the land of Egypt, out of the house of bondage." The children of Israel had lived under the rule of a man who had killed their male babies, subjected them to cruel and unusual punishment and to harsh labor. Yet they refused to repent from their sins and return to God, their Redeemer. But they continued to groan under the pressure and cry unto Moses for deliverance. And God spoke to Moses saying:

"And I have also heard the groaning of the children of Israel, whom the Egyptians keep in bondage; and I have remembered my covenant. Wherefore say unto the children of Israel, I *am* the LORD, and I will rid you out of their bondage, and I will redeem you with an outstretched arm, and with great judgments" (Exodus 6:5, 6).

The children of Israel had been subjected to hard labor by Pharaoh's orders. Pharaoh worked God's people like animals. He looked at them as nothing more than a team of mules used to pull or draw heavy brick and mortar to build his beautiful palace. They worked with crossbars across their shoulders, carrying heavy substances to assist in building. They were whipped and beaten and made to work long days. They were depressed and oppressed; their ability to think for themselves was suppressed by an oppressor named Pharaoh. The yoke of bondage placed on them by Pharaoh was grievous and the people lived in constant fear of their taskmaster.

"Now there arose a new king over Egypt, which knew not Joseph. And said unto his people, Behold, the people of the children of Israel are more and mightier than we: Come on, let us deal wisely with them, lest they multiply, and it come to pass, that, when there falleth out any war, they join also unto our enemies, and fight against us, and so get them up out of the land. Therefore they did set over them taskmasters to afflict them with their burdens. And they built for Pharaoh treasure cities, Pithom and Raamses. But the more they afflicted them, the more they multiplied and grew. And they were grieved because of the children of Israel. And the Egyptians made the children of Israel to serve with rigour: And they made their lives bitter with hard with bondage, in morter, and in brick, and in all manner of service in the field: all their service, wherein they made them serve, was with rigour" (Exodus 1:8-14).

The people of Israel had sinned greatly against God. God understood their ways, and He knew the condition of their heart. He knew they were weak to their flesh. He knew they were unfaithful in their relationship with Him, and they worshipped other gods. Yet He loved them with a redeeming, compassionate and everlasting love. He desires to renew His covenant agreement with his people. "For I will have respect unto you, and make you fruitful, and multiply you and establish my covenant with you. And I will walk among you, and will be your God, and ye shall be my people" (Leviticus 26:9, 12).

God broke their yoke of bondage from Pharaoh, and he delivered them from their oppressor and out of the land of Egypt. "But God led the people about, through the way of the wilderness of the Red sea: and the children of Israel went up armed out of the land of Egypt" (Exodus 13:18). God continued to demonstrate His love of redemption, and He delivered the Israelites by drowning Pharaoh and his entire army in the Red Sea.

"And Moses said unto the people, Fear ye not, stand still, and see the salvation of the LORD, which he will shew you to day; for the Egyptians whom ye have seen today, ye shall see them again no more forever. And the LORD said unto Moses, Stretch out thine hand over the sea, that the waters may come again upon the Egyptians, upon their chariots, and upon their horsemen. And Moses stretched forth his hand over the sea, and the sea returned to his strength when the morning appeared; and the Egyptians fled against it; and the LORD overthrew the Egyptians in the midst of the sea. And the waters returned, and covered the chariots, and the horsemen, and all the host of Pharaoh that came into the sea after them; there remained not so much as one of them.

But the children of Israel walked upon dry land in the midst of the sea; and the waters were a wall unto them on their right hand, and on their left. Thus the LORD saved Israel that day out of the hand of the Egyptians; and Israel saw the Egyptians dead upon the sea shore" (Exodus 14:13, 26-30).

The people were so overjoyed, they sang a song to the Lord saying,

"I will sing unto the LORD, for he hath triumphed gloriously: the horse and his rider hath he thrown into the sea. The LORD is my strength and song, and he is become my salvation: he is my God, and I will prepare him an habitation; my father's God, and I will exalt him" (Exodus 15:1, 2).

But soon the people begin to murmur and complain against Moses. They soon lost sight of all God had done and began to worship other gods. And the people rejected the yoke of God for the yoke of man. They chose to take on the likeness of the Egyptians and created gods of gold made by men.

"And the LORD said unto Moses, Go, get thee down; for thy people, which thou broughtest out of the land of Egypt, have corrupted themselves: They have turned aside quickly out of the way which I commanded them: they have made a molten calf, and have worshipped it, and have sacrificed thereunto, and said, These be thy gods, O Israel, which have brought thee up out of the land of Egypt" (Exodus 32:7, 8).

God's wrath was kindled toward Israel.

What the children of Israel did not understand then and people still fail to understand today is that rejecting the yoke of God will only result in their bowing under an even heavier weight, burden and guilt of men that is heavier than the yoke of God. The new bondage imposed by God as a result of their rebellion is a *spiritual bondage* from which no man can deliver them.

"And the LORD said unto Moses, Whosoever hath sinned against me, him will I blot out of my book. Therefore now go, lead the people unto the place of which I have spoken unto thee…nevertheless in the day when I visit I will visit their sin upon them. And the LORD plagued the people, because they made the calf, which Aaron made" (Exodus 32:33-35).

"This is the ordinance of the law which the LORD hath commanded, saying, Speak unto the children of Israel, that they bring thee a red heifer without spot, wherein is no blemish, and upon which never came yoke" (Numbers 19:2).

God seeks those who will worship Him voluntarily and freely. He wants to have an intimate relationship with those who are bound to him by cords of love—not a crossbar and harness that forces them to pray and worship Him and not a yoke that is induced by what they can get from God. He wants a relationship with those who are compelled to pray and praise Him because they love Him. He wants to have a loving relationship with those who will give not grudgingly nor of necessity, for God loves a cheerful giver. He wants the one upon whom never came the yoke of grievousness in service and servanthood when operating in their God-given gifts, talents and abilities for the perfecting of the saints and edifying of the church.

When we choose man's yoke over the yoke of God, guilt, pain, suffering, fear and death is imminent. Pharaoh made it very clear he would not stop until the children of Israel were killed.

This biblical truth remains today:

"Because thou servedst not the LORD thy God with joyfulness, and with gladness of heart, for the abundance of things; Therefore shalt thou serve thine enemies which the LORD shall send against thee, in hunger, and in thirst, and in nakedness, and in want of all things: and he shall put a yoke of iron upon thy neck, until he have destroyed thee" (Deuteronomy 28:47, 48).

When you reject God's yoke, your enemies which have set their heart against you, will place a yoke around your neck that is so heavy and burdensome, it will destroy you. That yoke will keep you from walking into your divine destiny God has spoken over your life.

But God's yoke is easy, and His burden is light. God says:

"…Fear not: for I have redeemed thee, I have called thee by thy name; thou art mine. When thou passest through the waters, I will be with thee; and through the rivers, they shall not overflow thee; when thou walkest through the fire, thou shalt not be burned; neither shall flame kindle upon thee" (Isaiah 43:1, 2).

God's yoke is profitable "…for *reproof, for correction, for instruction in righteousness: That the man of God may be perfect, thoroughly furnished unto all good works*" (II Timothy 2:16, 17), producing total surrender and submission under the hand of God.

CHAPTER NINE

COME BEFORE WINTER

"Do thy diligence to come before winter..." (II Timothy 4:21).

Winter, the season of the year between autumn and spring, is characterized by coldness, misery, bareness or death. Autumn, the season between summer and winter, is characterized by a period of beauty and maturity, yet on the verge of decline. Spring, the season between winter and summer, is characterized by a period of new growth and renewal.

Paul wrote a letter to his dear friend, Timothy, who had intimately worked alongside of him during his second missionary journey as well as other visitations at Corinth, Macedonia, Ephesus and Jerusalem. Timothy was a trusted friend and a companion to Paul. As Paul closed his letter, he admonished Timothy to do diligence to come to him before *winter.*

Why does Paul place the emphasis on *winter?* I believe Paul's statement is parallel to the winter season or the period of time in the life of Christ. In the tenth chapter of John, Jesus encountered opposition from Jews as He walked in the temple in Solomon's porch.

"Then came the Jews round about him, and said unto him, How long dost thou make us to doubt? If thou be the Christ, tell us plainly. Jesus answered them, I told you, and ye believed not; the works that I do in my Father's name, they bear witness of me. But ye believe not, because ye are not of my sheep, as I said unto you. My sheep hear my voice, and I know them, and they follow me: And I give unto them eternal life; and they shall never perish, neither shall any *man* pluck them out of my hand. My Father, which gave them to me, is greater than all; and no *man* is able to pluck them out of my Father's hand. I and *my* Father are one. Then the Jews took up stones again to stone him" (John 10:24-31).

The feast of the dedication was going on while Jesus was there. This was a dedication feast that began in December in observance of the dedication of a new altar and purging of the temple after the original temple had been profaned and the altar been defiled. As Jesus was walking through the temple, He was accosted by some Jews and challenged to defend His position. Jesus had told the Jews over and over who He was and His purpose, and so it is today. But people create their own self-doubt because of their prejudices and denial of the truth. Then they cast blame on someone else other than themselves for their unbelief. This is what the Jews were attempting to do with Jesus. They blamed Jesus for their unbelief.

As a matter of fact, they really did not enquire because they sought knowledge to change their way of thinking. They asked the question to create doubt and confusion in the minds of others. They challenged Christ's deity and His authority...even after He had given them sufficient proof of His name and power. Jesus responded by giving them an illustration of His relationship to those who understood His biblical truths. He told them that He was the shepherd, and all the sheep that belong to the shepherd hear His voice.

Jesus was saying, "With hearing comes recognition of ownership and total obedience—*even unto death*. The sheep go where the shepherd instructs them." As their Shepherd, He tells them He has made great provisions for His sheep. Jesus' sheep are protected; they have eternal life, joy and preservation from hell. Their salvation is secure in Him and the Father.

Jesus responded that He and the Father are one. Jesus responded to the Jews' accusations by saying, "Say ye of him, whom the Father hath sanctified, and sent into the world, Thou blasphemest; because I said, I am the Son of God?" (v. 36). God sanctified and sent Jesus the Word as a representation of Himself. Therefore, Jesus has no restrictions of power, authority or territory.

Earlier Jesus told the disciples how He had the power to lay down His life and the power to take it again. No man has the power to take Christ's life. He tells them He had been commanded of God with this power and authority (vv. 17, 18). After declaring His divine deity, Jesus moved on, and John 13:1 states,

"Now before the feast of the Passover, when Jesus knew that his hour was come that he should depart out of this world unto the Father, having loved his own who were in the world, he loved them unto the end."

Winter had begun in the life of Jesus, just as it had in the life of Paul. Jesus wasted no time in teaching the disciples their final lessons.

Jesus took time to wash the disciples' feet to give the disciples a lesson on servanthood and humility. "After that he poureth water into a basin, and began to wash the disciples' feet, and to wipe them with the towel wherewith he was girded" (John 13:5). Jesus then told the disciples that one of them would betray him saying, "…Verily, verily, I say unto you, that one of you shall betray me" (John 13:21). Jesus comforted and reassured His disciples thereafter saying:

"Let not your heart be troubled: ye believe in God, believe also in me. In my Father's house are many mansions: if it were not so, I would have told you. I go to prepare a place for you. And if I go and prepare a place for you, I will come again, and receive you unto myself; that where I am, there ye may be also. And whither I go ye know, and the way ye know" (John 14:1-4).

The disciples learned an important illustration that helped them understand they were intricately interwoven with Christ. "I am the vine, ye are the branches: He that abideth in me, and I in him, the same bringeth forth much fruit: for without me ye can do nothing"

(John 15:5). He wanted them to be sure of their salvation in him and to know their salvation was eternal.

Not only did He reassure them of their position in Christ, He warned them of sure persecution because of their association with Christ. He told them His departure was needed in order to provide them with the power they would need to endure the persecution.

"These things have I spoken unto you, that ye should not be offended. They shall put you out of the synagogues: yea, the time cometh, that whosoever killeth you will think he doeth God service....Nevertheless I tell you the truth; it is expedient for you that I go away: for if I go not away, the Comforter will not come unto you; but if I depart, I will send him unto you" (John 16:1, 2, 7).

And finally, Jesus prayed for His beloved disciples because He knew what was ahead for them.

"I have manifested thy name unto the men which thou gavest me out of the world: thine they were, and thou gavest them me; and they have kept thy word. Now they have known that all things whatsoever thou hast given me are of thee. For I have given unto them the words which thou gavest me; and they received them, and have known surely that I came out from thee, and they have believed that thou didst send me. I pray for them: I pray not for the world, but for them which thou hast given me; for they are thine" (John 17:6-9).

Jesus was pleased to know He had accomplished the will of the Father. He needed the disciples to hear the prayer He was praying to the Father on their behalf and the behalf of those who would come after them, so they would be encouraged. Jesus prayed for all those who were in the Father's hand, that man was unable to pluck out.

Jesus knew He was in His winter season. He knew death was near, and little time was left to teach the disciples. Jesus wanted to move the disciples to the level of maturity they would need in order to serve Him faithfully after His death.

Shortly after Jesus prayed for the disciples, he was betrayed by Judas, arrested and was led before Pilate for trial.

"Then led they Jesus from Caiaphas unto the hall of judgment: and it was early; and they themselves went not into the judgment hall, lest they should be defiled; but that they might eat the passover. Pilate then went out unto them, and said, What accusation bring ye against this man? (John 18:28, 29).

"Then Pilate therefore took Jesus, and scourged him" (John 19:1).

"Then delivered he him therefore unto them to be crucified. And they took Jesus, and led him away. And he bearing the cross went forth into a place called *the place* of a skull, which is called in Hebrew Golgotha: Where they crucified him, and two others with him, on either side one, and Jesus in the midst" (John 19:16-18).

Jesus knew He would soon return to rapture His church, and we too, like the disciples, have but a short time to prepare for His return. We have just a short while to seek our opportunities for spiritual growth and maturity in Him. The lost have but a little while to accept His salvation of eternal life in exchange of eternal damnation.

Winter was a difficult season in Jesus' life. It was a season of agony and pain. He longed to be with the Father, yet He knew He would have to endure the physical pain and suffering on the cross in order to complete the final task the Father had assigned.

Paul, Hosea, Job, David, Mary and Martha, Joseph, Naomi and Ruth all knew too well what it meant to enter into the *winter* season of life. They had to *sort through God's love* through their personal circumstances to discover God's redeeming love before *winter* was over. They had tasks to complete and obligations to meet before *winter* ended. They knew at some point they would not see another spring.

And so it is today. *Winter* will come into the life of every man, woman, boy and girl. There will be no opportunity for growth and renewal. Winter has no respect of age, race, creed or color. Every living soul will eventually experience *winter*.

God used all of these people from chapter one through chapter nine, and He still uses people today to demonstrate His love to, for and toward His children. He used the characters we have studied throughout these chapters to prepare us for *winter*. He used the Old Testament saints to prepare the hearts and mind of His people, not only to receive His Son, but to understand the sacrifice of His Son. God wants us to understand His heart and mind through the lives of people whom we can see, hear and touch. God used each one of these saints and the Lord Jesus Christ to draw us to Him.

God manifested Himself in His Son to show us who He is. Yes, *God loves you*. He sacrificed His only Son to demonstrate His love for you. He loves you so much He is willing to subject you to His divine *testing and discipline of delay* to produce Godly character in you. He wants you to understand His love will never die, and it covers a multitude of sins.

Why does God love you? Because you were created in His image, and in spite of how much it hurts, He knows *it's a good thing that we suffer* in His will. He knows we will emerge with a firm affirmation of our declaration to *bless God at all times* because we know and believe *He's got our back*. He knows every experience will have been worth it when we can stand and say, *"His yoke is easy*; His burden is light."

So He sent His Son, and the Son gave His life that we might have a right to the tree of life. We hung Him high and stretched Him wide on the cross at Calvary. Jesus hung His head, and for you and me He died. But that's actually not how the story ends! Three days later Jesus rose again, declaring all power in heaven and earth are in His hands. Jesus reigns! *Yes*, Jesus reigns!

So *come…* Come to God through His Son, Jesus Christ. *Come before winter*. God is watching and waiting. The Spirit of the Lord says, "Come! Come! *Come before winter…*

ABOUT THE AUTHOR

Belinda F. Payne has been anointed with a gift from God to spread His Word through the ministries of speaking, teaching and writing. She is an anointed and dynamic speaker who has a passion for proclaiming the Gospel of Jesus Christ.

She is an author of books and articles. Belinda's work includes *'In the Garden'* and *'Sorting Through God's Love'* and many other short writings.

She is very passionate about the word of God. Belinda loves studying the word of God and teaching others about the word and work of the Lord Jesus Christ. She has served as a key conference and retreat speaker on numerous occasions.

Belinda currently presents the word of God in assisted living centers along with her husband Alvin in their ministry known as Bethesda2Ministries.

Bethesda2Ministries

Bethesda2Ministries was founded by Reverend Alvin Payne Jr. God's plan was for Alvin and Belinda to form a mobile church providing hope and spiritual healing in the lives of those living in assisted living centers through the preaching and teaching the gospel of Jesus Christ.

Bethesda2Ministries is a ministry of hope and healing and one that believes God remembers those others forget. Under the Leadership of Reverend Alvin Payne Jr. Bethesda2Ministries is devoted to spreading the gospel of Jesus Christ through biblical preaching, teaching, praise, and worship to those who desire salvation, spiritual growth, encouragement, strength and spiritual healing by the power and word of God. The Ministry focus is to bring the church to those that are unable to attend local church services in their communities.

Bethesda2Ministries is devoted to strengthening the faith, and hope of believers as they learn how to practically apply Jesus' teachings to their lives and present the plan of salvation to those who have not accepted Jesus Christ as their Lord and Savior. Attendees are invited to sit under sound doctrinal teaching with an ear to hear the voice of God, receive into their hearts the word of God, then learn how to practically apply the word in their daily living.

Upcoming Book: In the Garden

No more masks. No more veils. No more pretending. No more walls. No more excuses. Where is your garden? Sure, it's scary and it is also painful, but it will be worth it. Do you know where to find the peace, joy, and deliverance for which you have been longing?

I cannot count the times I faced burning bushes in my pathway. As I look back I am saddened by the fact that I either turned back, or I chose to go around my burning bushes never stopping long enough to listen to the voice of God for instructions, all because of fear.

You cannot begin to understand how much time I have wasted.

Join me for my next book - In the Garden – to be released in March 2019 and experience below the surface heart to heart devotions that will inspire and motivate you, to love you! Get ready to read this short but prolific writing that will change your life. How do I know? Because they changed mine!

Made in the USA
Middletown, DE
25 February 2019